Guidance
from the
Darkness

Guidance from the Darkness

How to Thrive

Through Difficult

Times

Mary Murray Shelton

Jeremy P. Tarcher/Penguin
a member of Penguin Group (USA) Inc., New York

This book, while based on true incidents, is not meant to betray any professional or personal confidences. Therefore, I have taken the liberty of changing the names and minor details of personal stories to protect the privacy of those involved.

Most Tarcher/Penguin books are available at special quantity discounts for bulk purchase for sales promotions, premiums, fund-raising, and educational needs. Special books or book excerpts also can be created to fit specific needs. For details, write Penguin Group (USA) Inc. Special Markets, 375 Hudson Street, New York, NY 10014.

Jeremy P. Tarcher/Penguin
a member of
Penguin Group (USA) Inc.
375 Hudson Street
New York, NY 10014
www.penguin.com

First trade paperback edition 2004
Copyright © 2000 by Mary Murray Shelton

The Library of Congress cataloged the hardcover edition as follows:

Shelton, Mary Murray, date.
Guidance from the darkness : the transforming power of the divine
feminine in difficult times / Mary Murray Shelton.
p.   cm.
ISBN 1-58542-003-4
1. Suffering—Religious aspects—Christianity.   2. Hope—Religious
aspects—Christianity.   3. Consolation.   4. Femininity of God.   I. Title.
BV4909.S49   2000   99-39394 CIP
299′.93—dc21

ISBN 1-58542-369-6 (paperback edition)

Printed in the United States of America
1   3   5   7   9   10   8   6   4   2

Book design by Chris Welch

Acknowledgments

....

My heartfelt gratitude to Joel Fotinos, my publisher, whose loving pursuit of this book worked miracles. I am grateful, too, for the clarity, depth of detail, and excellence that my editor, Wendy Hubbert, has added to the work. Barbara Moulton, my agent, provided much-needed guidance and support in getting things going on the right track. Her faith in me was a huge help. I am also honored by and appreciative of all the people whose stories appear in *Guidance from the Darkness*. I find their courage and ability to choose the compassionate and transformative path in the midst of their own darkness is inspiring and nourishing.

I also want to thank those women whose lives and work have helped me understand more about the Divine Feminine and Its connection with the darkness: Leslie McIntyre, Alexandra Cock, Susan Collins, Rev. Jody Miller Stevenson, Rev. Karyl Huntley, Rev. Sage Bennet, Sherry Ruth Anderson and Patricia Hopkins, Angeles Arrien, Jean Shinoda

Bolen, Carol Christ, Riane Eisler, Clarissa Pinkola Estés, Demetra George, Joan Halifax, Jennifer James, Anne Wilson Schaef, Merlin Stone, and Marion Woodman.

Lastly, my deepest gratitude goes to my family at home, whose loving encouragement and enthusiasm through many months of writing have fueled my passion to bring these ideas to the page.

For Amanda and Luke, who make me laugh, give me strength, and remind me of the Truth during my challenges. Your love and lives bring me amazing gifts.

Contents

....

Foreword

....

You are about to read a book that will forever change the way you cope with the dark moments in your life. Every one of us has experienced profound loss at one time or another — the death of a loved one, divorce, devastating illness, or a shattered dream. At times, it feels as if our heart will break from the sheer weight of misery and disappointment.

We can take all the pain and curse it, nurse it, and rehearse it. We can swallow a bitter pill every day to make us try to feel good about feeling bad. We can shrink from others, building a dense wall of isolation that protects us from ever having to hurt that way again. We can rage in perpetuity that life didn't turn out the way we expected.

Or, we can learn from Mary Murray Shelton's wisdom and do something better. Mary is no Pollyanna. She doesn't dismiss human pain, like those well-meaning friends who pat us on the shoulder and say, "Try to look on the bright side." Mary has walked through her own darkness and knows how easily hopelessness and fear can invade the heart. She would never tell us that bad things don't happen. What Mary believes is that it is in our bleakest hour when magic *does* happen.

We all have read about remarkable people who turned personal tragedy into triumph and in so doing have offered a great gift to the world. Mahatma Gandhi, the Reverend Martin Luther King, Jr., and, of course, the Master Jesus come to mind. Mary's belief is that we, as ordinary individuals, possess the same inner power to relieve pain and increase happiness, not just for ourselves but for others.

As Mary says, we never know what's coming next, so how can we say that a shattering experience today won't contribute to an unforeseen blessing tomorrow? The only difference between seizing the blessing and missing it lies entirely in how we look at the experience. And she shows us where to look. With wisdom, insight, and humor, Mary intimately shares her own experience and walks us through the process that leads from unimaginable darkness to brilliant light.

Mary and I share not only our names and profession but a deep belief in the power of Spirit to heal the most devastating of the heart's wounds. I first heard of Mary in the early 1990s as "that minister in northern California everyone is talking about." Her messages to her congregation were moving, powerful, and relevant. People were packed to the rafters to hear what she had to say. I knew then that I wanted to meet her. When we did meet at the ordination ceremony for a mutual friend, I was struck by the power of Mary's presence. Clearly, this was a woman gifted both in wisdom and grace.

I'll always remember watching Mary sit with a woman who had been abandoned by the love of her life and who had lost the job of her dreams, both in less than a month. The woman later told me that she had felt that her life was over, but through her minister's gentle encouragement and powerful teaching, the woman went on to find within herself the seeds of a new beginning. She built a highly successful business and found a relationship that satisfied her soul. Her life hadn't been over; with Mary's help, she was led to a greater beginning.

I knew then that one day Reverend Mary Murray Shelton must share her tremendous vision of hope with the world. And now she has.

—Mary Manin Morrissey
Founder and Senior Minister of
the Living Enrichment Center
Author of *Building Your Field of Dreams* and
Finding Perfect Love in Imperfect Relationships

Introduction

In a dark time, the eye begins to see.
— *Theodore Roethke*

The expression "dark night of the soul," coined by St. John of the Cross, is one we all seem to relate to, even without knowing the personal journey to which St. John was referring. Pain is a universal human experience. While it has many different textures and characters, pain spares no one. All of us encounter deep pain at some time in our lives, and whether that pain is physical, mental, or emotional, it often brings us to a crisis of suffering. Crises like these — stemming from the loss of a loved one, a job, or one's health, for example — I call experiences of the darkness. These experiences provide us with an opening, a possibility for transformation, that few other things in life do. This is not to suggest that we need to suffer to grow but rather to point out something we often miss about our most challenging experiences: pain has the potential to grab our attention like nothing else and to change us in deep, important, and permanent ways.

Much of how we experience such a crisis depends upon

our attitude toward it, our expectations of its outcome, and the way in which we allow ourselves to receive guidance and support to know what to do. It isn't pain that differentiates us from one another, but our *response* to that pain.

Personally, and in years of working with congregants in pastoral care situations, I've observed both the extraordinary breakthroughs that can come with these experiences and, in some cases, the extraordinary destruction. The difference that sets outcomes in motion is not external but internal, in the way a person chooses to interpret his or her pain.

Darkness entered my life early. My adored father, a heavy smoker, died of a stroke ten days after my third birthday. Entering elementary school in the fifties without a father at home was a lot like walking around with a visible scar or limp. I thought my friends saw me as an oddity, and their parents pitied me. I grieved as some children do, alone at night in the dark, bargaining with God in tears to bring my father back to me. As an adult, I've come to realize that there are things I learned and strengths I possess today that directly benefit the work I love to do, which developed as a result of coping with the loss of my father. This does not undo the grief I felt because of his absence; rather, it recognizes that the experience also brought with it new possibilities.

Over the years as a minister and a friend, I've been honored to share with others some of their own dark times. A man dying of cancer. A woman going through a divorce. A fellow battling addiction. A couple whose investments were wiped out right before retirement. Parents whose two daughters committed suicide in the same year. In many of these encounters I have seen individuals respond in inspiring, powerful ways to such challenges in spite of the depth of pain involved. I have seen their lives after the event changed as a result of how they chose to respond during the event.

Through my own experiences and those of my congregants, I've learned that there is a magic that can come in times of darkness and despair. Not everyone can see it. Sometimes we find it almost impossible to get enough distance from the pain to let the magic in. But for those who open to it, peace and light enter their lives at a fuller, richer level than ever before, and they are changed. I call this magic the Divine Feminine. In this book, the term *Divine Feminine* refers to an innate wisdom within us that we can tap into, as well as the feminine aspect of the Presence of God, which can guide us. This feminine aspect of God is referred to in most of the world's great religious traditions and cultures. She has many names and many roles. In Mexico, one of her aspects is that of Coatlicue, known as the Mother of God and as the filth eater; in India, Kali, the destroyer; in Judaism, the Shekinah, the embodiment of the Divine within the world and its people; in Christianity, Mary, the Mother of God; in some Native American traditions, the Corn Goddess; in China, Quan Yin, the Goddess of Compassion; in ancient earth-based worship traditions, Inanna, Queen of Heaven. And there are many, many more. As I speak of it, this Divine Feminine is within, around, and beyond us. And while it is available as a resource for us to draw from, it also prods us to blossom into our fullest potential and, sometimes, pushes us to our limits and beyond in order to break through into that potential. Opening to the Divine Feminine can be the key to unlocking the new meaning in the darkness we experience, for that darkness is also the home of our creativity. Learning to surrender to that creative inner power in times when crisis catapults us into the unknown can lead to amazing personal transformation.

We are all familiar with the masculine aspects of the Divine, which have been emphasized in Western culture: God as Father, King of Heaven, Ruler of the Universe, giver of laws, judge, and dispenser of punishment. But we have largely lost track of a daily sense of some of the feminine aspects of the Divine: the Mother, nonlinear, nurturing, intuitive, healing, and life-giving. I believe that human beings contain all the aspects of the Creator, and that we may directly experience the Divine Feminine within us and benefit from that inner wisdom, both in times of active seeking and in times when it comes to us apparently unbidden. For many people, it is during times of darkness that the Divine Feminine can be felt, and the Guidance it brings can be perceived and followed more easily. The Divine Feminine isn't there only in times of darkness, but we seem to be more receptive to it when everything we usually rely upon has crumbled.

Society, or our families, may support us in believing such times are someone else's fault, God's will, or a result of our own ineptitude. These common interpretations can leave us with guilt, emptiness, bitterness, or an excuse to lay blame, but none of these urges us forward or brings us peace. This book offers an alternative interpretation of what is happening to us during experiences of darkness. Looking at these experiences in a different way can offer hope, a way to cope with the experience while still in the process of living through it, and a way to understand the changes you may undergo in its aftermath. The difficult events and experiences in our lives are true opportunities for us to move forward in profound and personal ways. But if we never know this, we may have only common interpretations to fall back on, leaving us feeling incomplete and stuck.

An unknown element comes with the onset of these experiences of darkness. This is Guidance from the Divine Feminine, but it doesn't usually look like what we expect Divine Guidance to look like. It often steers us toward a risk of some sort that we would not choose on our own. We are urged in times of crisis to go into the unknown and trust the outcome to this divine unpredictable energy. This type of Guidance is intuitive, powerful, nonlinear, uncontrollable. It can feel frightening, because what it asks of us is frightening.

To the degree that most of us are control freaks, being asked to make a new choice without a security net is reason enough to be rattled. Yet time and time again, I have seen that by making the frightening choice a sufferer is guided to make, she is led into new realms of power, love, beauty, strength, and success that she would never have accessed from the manner in which she habitually lived her life up to that moment.

This interpretation is not widely known or discussed, and

that's a shame. People need to have a deeper understanding of their experiences of darkness and the potential such experiences offer for amazing personal transformation. We need this higher awareness so that we can respond differently in our own times of pain and crisis by increasing our willingness to open to and trust the Guidance that comes to us during the dark times and brings soothing to the pain.

Guidance is always there, even when the direction it suggests is not what we think we want to follow. Usually we are looking for Guidance that will show us how to stop the pain as soon as possible or give us easy answers that will maintain the status quo. These are things that won't challenge us, things that won't push us to change. But that isn't the primary role of Guidance from the Divine Feminine. Its role is, instead, to show us how we *must* change in order to transform the habitual patterns of our lives. As we surrender to that change, the things we need to know and do in order to cope with the pain and to bring healing to it also show up to provide us with a path back to wholeness.

Understanding the need for change is not the same thing as knowing how to go about effecting it. In this first part of the book you'll learn how darkness can provide an opening to greater light through the stories of people who have experienced it. The second part of the book explores how to approach our experiences of darkness by using eight tools that I call Qualities of Being: attention, intention, choice, practice, surrender, intuition, gratitude, and trust. Each of these tools contains two aspects: attitude and action. Choosing to apply these Qualities of Being requires most of us to change our customary attitudes toward painful situations, as well as our ways of handling them. The qualities require us to see things in a new way and practice new actions, and these are essential to real transformation. Such practices transform both the internal idea and the external experience of who we are. Our very being seems new.

Many of us know what it's like to try to lose weight, only to gain all of it back. We have changed our behavior without changing our thoughts, so the change is only temporary. Likewise, we've all met people who don't seem to practice what they advise others to do. They have the right ideas but don't put them into action, and so nothing changes in their outer world, either. Behavior and thought both must be changed in order to bring about permanent change in our lives. When put into practice, Qualities of Being can transform the way we see and experience pain and darkness, as well as our behavior while in the midst of them. They are the tools we can use on a daily basis to make our necessary changes permanent.

This approach to times of darkness is profound, going beyond relieving the symptom of pain to address its deeper causes. It allows an inner divine wisdom to custom-make for us a real healing for our painful situations, and, in this way, we don't handle one painful situation only to create another one for ourselves the next year. Through the Guidance of the Divine Feminine, we learn to listen to the darkness itself and find the key to freedom that is waiting for us there. By applying the Qualities of Being to our situation, we actively use that key to transform ourselves. Like learning to use any tool, we usually don't begin to practice Qualities of Being with ease and perfection. Imagine the first time you tried to use a computer, a hammer, or a knife. As awkward as mastering them may initially be, learning to use tools ultimately makes our lives easier and more productive, once we've discovered how to use them properly and practiced enough to become proficient. What is difficult to do correctly at first eventually becomes easy, and so helpful that we can't imagine not ever having been able to use these tools to accomplish our tasks. The same is true of learning how to apply the Qualities of Being—expect to be awkward at first, but persist, realizing that the skills you develop in learning to apply these spiritual tools will make your life easier in the long run.

In experiencing difficult times, you stand on the brink of limitless new possibilities. If you are challenged in your life today by some loss or sadness, I invite you to enter that darkness with me now and find the Guidance from the Divine Feminine that is waiting there for you. Glimpse possibilities that can change your life, and learn to use the Qualities of Being to come through this time of darkness transformed. Let this time of breaking down become a time of breaking through.

Part One

EXPERIENCES OF
DARKNESS

One

Change Is a Process, Not an Event

....

Nature will not let us stay in any one place too long. She will let us stay just long enough to gather the experience necessary to the unfolding and advancement of the soul. This is a wise provision, for should we stay here too long, we would become too set, too rigid, too inflexible. Nature demands change in order that we may advance.

—*Ernest Holmes,* The Science of Mind

Change affects us all. Events happen in our lives and changes result, not only externally but internally, because change encompasses more than the events themselves; it includes our responses and our reactions to those events over time. The initial event has an immediate effect on us, and we have a response to that impact. But it isn't just the moment of impact that we respond to. We continue to respond, over time, to our memory of the event and to the sequence of unfoldments that follows. This whole change process influences our perception of life as we know it. The country-western singer Kathy Mattea sings, "I loved life as we knew it, I still can't believe we threw it away. Good-bye, that's all there is to it: life as we knew it ended today."

Because the effect of a particular event alters life as we know it, it sets into motion a sequence of unfoldments. These unfoldments are our sequential responses to the event, as well as to our own previous responses, and the responses of other people. An example would be the way one's thoughts and feelings might change about the initiating event as time goes on. When a relationship breaks up, the partner on the receiving end may initially feel hurt, and later move toward being very nice and cooperative in an attempt to be taken back. When this fails, the individual may begin to feel very angry, both at the leaving partner and at himself for his previous behavior during the breakup. He may act out this anger, attacking his former partner verbally. This may be followed by feelings of remorse and regret that spill over from current behavior to memories of other past relationships that didn't work out. Each feeling and action are part of a sequence of unfoldments in the change process for that particular individual experiencing the breakup. As you can see, they aren't logically linear, though each relates to the others. Sometimes they overlap or backtrack, and usually they get messy.

We enter into a process as a result of that initial event. I am calling this process a sequence of unfoldments. We usually respond to that impact and enter the sequence of unfoldments that follows it unconsciously, from habit.

When we fall in love, have a baby, lose a job, or let go of a loved one, our first response tends to be the automatic response we've been socialized to expect to have. We feel happy, we feel sad, we feel excited, we feel scared, we feel angry. But we can also have a response to those events that is chosen. To the degree that we can consciously choose our response to change, we're present in the experience in the moment. When our action is governed by habit, our attention is elsewhere: on the past, on the future, on other people's responses. When it is intentionally chosen, our attention is with the experience of the present moment. This allows us more freedom to respond in a way that relates appropriately to the current circumstances. Choices occur throughout the sequence of unfoldments. As each unfoldment arises, we may respond automatically from habit, or choose to really look at the opportunity before us to discover what the best response might be. When we choose to consider alternatives to our habits, we invite the Divine Feminine—that inner, intuitive knowing—to guide us toward the best choice.

A particular sequence of unfoldments begins with an event that changes the status quo. Such a change usually initiates grief, the first unfoldment in the sequence, because the familiar, to which we are attached, must be released. Grieving requires time, but eventually a small measure of familiarity with the new circumstances begins to take hold, and we may choose to start to return to a more normal flow of life. We become aware, the second unfoldment in the sequence, that new life is emerging and that we are being called to enter into it actively.

Our willingness to look deeply into the new and come to trust it enough to prepare to enter in is the third unfoldment. The fourth unfoldment is the action that emerges from that willingness. If we choose to enter the new, the unknown, and actively discover what our part is in this new way of life, our choice will trigger the fifth unfoldment: struggle.

Because we are redefining life and our place in it, there is confusion in the sorting out. There is a struggle between what was and what is becoming. In order to enter into the new, one must be able to let go of the aspects of the old that no longer serve. Some of those are internal aspects of ourselves, and letting go of parts of ourselves usually entails struggle. If we see the struggle through to resolution, it leads to the concluding unfoldment in the sequence: when the struggle resolves, we discover ourselves as new beings or, more accurately, as more complete beings—*transformed*. The potential for this newness was always within us; we were simply unaware of it until the time for it was ripe.

This entire sequence of unfoldments is one of the natural expressions of the Divine Feminine: change itself, in its mysterious, unpredictable, nonlogical occurrence, is an aspect of the nonlinear, holistic divinity within us. Change need not be the destruction we often perceive it to be. Rather, it can be our opportunity to evolve into the next phase of our fullest expression of self, and when we do so in cooperation with the process itself, the greater Self within us, this expression of the Divine, is revealed and allowed to do its work.

At each unfoldment in this sequence, the Divine Feminine can be felt as its influence is brought to bear on us, guiding us toward the right choices via our intuition—that sense of inner knowing. Along the way, we can choose at each point to continue moving toward the new, or to fall back on habits rather than complete the process. Our choices determine who we will have become when the dust has settled.

Let's look at the unfoldments in more detail.

When a momentous event hits, it's like a meteor landing in our life. Whether the event is positive or negative, one of the components that follows its impact is often grief. Have you ever experienced the blues after achieving a long anticipated goal? Perhaps it is because achieving it means that now you must let go of life as you have known it. Even a good event creates a feeling of loss because of its effect on the familiar. A promotion; a new relationship; a move to another part of the country where you've always wanted to live, all require letting go of something familiar. So the first unfoldment in our process of change is grief.

We might stay in that unfoldment for any length of time. The need to grieve a change is natural and human and healthy. Each of us is unique in the amount of time that we need to grieve. For major losses like the death of a spouse, a minimum of two years of grief seems to be the norm. When grief comes, its first effects can be confusing. We may feel numb, alternating with waves of raw emotion. Sometimes it seems we're fine, then depression comes. We can't concentrate well, become forgetful, have no appetite, sleep poorly. Some of us think we're going crazy when these things happen, particularly if our intellect has always been a source of direction and comfort. It seems the intellect cannot grasp the idea of a permanent loss. The idea of forever is beyond true understanding, and when a permanent loss alters our lives, the intellect tends to shut off and leave us only with a sort of automatic pilot. The automatic pilot gets us to work on time, but we may not remember how we got there, or if we had breakfast, showered, or even dressed.

When my husband and I were divorced, this is exactly how the grief affected me. I managed the everyday things that needed to be done. I bought groceries, prepared meals, bathed my son, got him to school, went to work. But I felt hollow inside—empty. At other times I felt overwhelming grief. I couldn't understand how the sun could continue to shine as if everything were fine, when my life had been smashed to smithereens. It took quite a while before my emotions and thinking began to feel really familiar—over a year, in fact. And that is when I began to come back to life.

Grief is a release of energy that opens the way to letting go of something or someone or some circumstance to which we are attached. Without the grieving, we never seem to fully let go, thereby never becoming fully free to enter into the new. But grief is not meant to be hopelessness. When the attachment energy begins to be diminished through the expression of grief over time, we begin to lose grieving momentum. We look up out of ourselves and see the world again. We begin to realize there are things, people, circumstances, beyond the ones we lost, which may need us in some way.

Two women I knew in Seattle had lost children in automobile collisions with drunk drivers. One remained angry, never resolving her grief, and used the pain as an excuse to indulge her own drug problem. Another struggled with her loss, found a way through the grief, finally, and turned to her art to communicate the importance of forgiveness between individuals and nations. One chose her habit, the other a new approach to her crushing loss.

This dawning awareness that we are being called out of our grief usually begins to happen in us spontaneously. Spontaneity itself is another aspect of the Divine Feminine. We can't predict when the time will be right, but when it is, we will know it. We may or may not feel ready for it, and this may determine our willingness to respond affirmatively to life's invitation to reenter the stream of activity fully.

At some point, life starts to give us clues, little opportunities to look up out of that experience of grief and make ourselves available to the shift that happens as our grief diminishes. We can ignore the clues and choose grief as a way of life, or we can pay attention to those clues. Usually we don't take the first opportunity. Life may be tapping on our shoulder for a while before we realize that opportunities to shift are showing up. Our clear realization is the beginning of awareness.

I was in my final year of ministerial training when my husband and I separated. It was the hardest year of my life. After graduation, I spent six months simply going to work, and being with my son and roommates at home. Then I began to feel antsy to get on with my ministry, and slowly I began to prepare my résumé, photographs, audiotapes of sermons I'd given, and cover letters to send to churches who were seeking ministers. I felt less raw, less off-center, and more prepared to take up life again. I was becoming impatient with the status quo. I was spending more and more time thinking about the possibilities for my ministry. This was my entry into awareness, the next unfoldment in the sequence that follows grief.

When we first begin to be aware that there are opportunities to shift out of grief and reenter life, we may find that we resist them. We may even respond with self-righteous indignation at the very suggestion that we might be done with grieving. But life will insistently begin to provide us with reminders to look up out of our grieving and make ourselves available for a new opportunity. Eventually, if we do, Life takes hold of us and draws our attention further away from the grief and back into life. It "calls our name." And if we listen to that calling and come forward, we move into the next unfoldment in the sequence. This is the beginning of willingness.

When I began to be bored with grieving the loss of the marriage dream—telling the story, going through the memories and feelings—I began to be more aware of the present and future than the past, and my life could go forward again. I began to make plans. This was the beginning of the third unfoldment for me. I was willing to be an active participant in things again. I began to notice, with interest, opportunities to participate in, and contribute to, life. As I became aware of these opportunities, I discovered that some things seemed too demanding for me, while others looked like fun. Those that were both enticing and within my capacity began to get my attention, and I pursued these, eventually being ready for interviews at various churches and being hired as minister at one of them in northern California. For me, this was the beginning of action, the fourth unfoldment in the sequence.

When we become willing, ready or not, we are expressing yet another natural aspect of the Divine Feminine: opening to and trusting the unknown. The Divine Feminine is the home of the mystery—that which we do not yet know. When we choose to trust that newness and open ourselves to it, we are immersing ourselves in the Divine Feminine and surrendering to its Guidance.

What automatically follows willingness is action. This action doesn't arise out of a carefully planned list of goals. It arises, rather, out of an inner feeling that "it's time." And the action that is chosen arises from the center of our being with a feeling that can be a mixture of impulsion and knowingness that this is the thing to do. Action emerging out of knowingness, rather than intellectual analysis, is motivated by the Divine Feminine within us — that aspect of ourselves that simply *knows*. We may not be able to explain how we know, but we feel it strongly nevertheless. It is the intuitive part of our being that is leading the way.

The action that we choose as a result of awareness and willingness determines our experience of an event and the impact it has on our lives. When grief has finally spent itself and we are invited to look at life around us again, we always have the option to look away from the present and spend our energy brooding over the past. Essentially this is the choice to continue to hold the life-is-over view. Our awareness has been pulled toward life, but we are unwilling to participate. We take no new action. We try to keep our lives as much like the past as we can, perhaps hoping to re-create that past once again, though this is never possible. A life that stops here is sluggish and lacks vision. Fewer and fewer possibilities are even noticed. The present becomes a museum to the past.

If and when we choose to take up life again, we actively make choices that take us into the future, into newness. Moses is an archetypal example of one's change process being expressed through the unfoldments of grief, awareness, willingness, and action. Moses had killed an Egyptian soldier who was abusing Hebrew slaves, and he had gone into hiding in fear for his life. He fled from his place in Egypt as one of Pharaoh's chosen ones, and while in hiding in Midian, he married the daughter of a priest named Jethro, and began shepherding his father-in-law's sheep. There he grieved his loss of position, freedom, and respect.

One day when he was out in the fields, he happened to look up and see a bush that was on fire but was not being consumed by the flame. The order of events that follow that moment in the story is important, because the progression reaffirms the sequence of our own unfoldments in the process of change. The Book of Exodus says, "And the angel of the Lord appeared to him in a flame of fire out of the midst of a bush. And he looked and beheld the bush was on fire and the bush was not consumed. And Moses said, I will now turn aside and see this great sight, why the bush is not burned. And when the Lord saw that he turned aside to see, God called him out of the midst of the bush and said, 'Moses, Moses,' And he said, 'Here am I.' "

In this short three-verse passage, Moses makes three decisions. The first is to be aware of life around him, and in order to do this, he has to set aside his preoccupation with grief. First, he looks at the bush. Granted, the burning bush was designed to get his attention and he would have had to be completely preoccupied with himself not to notice that a nearby bush was on fire. But how many of us overlook something as obvious as a burning bush when we are really wrapped up in ourselves? There are times when I could overlook a whole forest fire.

The burning bush catches Moses' awareness, and he chooses to give his attention to it. That choice—willingness—is his second decision. He says to himself, "I will turn aside and see this wonder, see why this bush is not consumed." Meanwhile, the Infinite is waiting. Watching. "Is Moses going to notice? Good, he noticed. Is he going to pay attention? Yes, here he comes." Then God calls to him *by name*, and Moses makes the third decision — action — by responding to the call. The call itself signals the coming change in his life from a time of grieving to a time of newness. Moses chooses to participate in whatever comes next when he answers, "Here am I."

In the first unfoldment of the change process, we may feel unfinished with sadness and mourning, but the Infinite never gives up on us. Next time it will be a bigger bush with a louder voice until, for many of us, it becomes irresistible, and we respond, saying, "Here I am." By the time we're ready to do so, we will answer almost without thinking because we are so ripe to go forward into the newness. This is the phase of the change process when we take action.

It would be pleasant for us if taking action were the end of the change process, but there is more. Action motivated from inner knowing arises from the mystery itself — the Divine Feminine — and it challenges the way we have defined ourselves up to that time. A struggle usually ensues in which who we have been resists the change being motivated by who we are becoming. The two identities "wrestle" with each other to determine which will be the Self that continues from that moment on.

The Guidance of the Divine Feminine has brought us to the

place of wrestling, and the courage that emerges from staying with the struggle until it is resolved and allowing the new to emerge is powerful indeed. Emerging from that struggle is a little like being a chick who has successfully emerged from the shell: the struggle empowers us for life. This is the most personally transformative part of the change process. In the book *The Life We Are Given* by George Leonard and Michael Murphy, Leonard states, "Your resistance to change is likely to reach its peak when significant change is imminent." This uncomfortable experience of resistance is what I mean by wrestling.

Several years ago I saw a play in which the main character was offered an opportunity to step forward in his life into newness. The opportunities came to make his talent as an entertainer available in the world in a larger way and, in so doing, also to take hold of the love that he'd always wanted in his life. His own inner doubts surrounded him onstage like other characters, saying, "Who do you think you are? That's not you. This isn't your place." He listened to those voices, turned away from his possible future, and went back to who he had been.

When I was leaving the theater after the performance, a friend commented, "Well, that wasn't very inspirational!" We had both been hoping that this character would take the opportunity to respond to the call as a result of his inner struggle. There is something in us that wants to see people make the choices that really will forward them in their lives. And so the Divine Feminine is with us. It nudges and pushes us to make those choices for growth and newness as irresistible as possible, but the choice is still up to us.

The story of Jacob in the Bible also illustrates the struggle that is the fifth unfoldment in this change process. Initially Jacob seems to be favored by God, and he is certainly his mother's favorite. But he does some shady things. He steals the birthright from his brother, Esau, who is none too happy about it. He surreptitiously takes a lot of land, cattle, and possessions from his father-in-law. This is who Jacob is, this is how he has lived his life by habit. But it's time for change. Something motivates him to go back to the land where Esau lives and make peace with him. Wisely, he's a little nervous about it.

Have you ever had a falling-out with a family member in which you have behaved particularly badly and you're making the first approach toward reconciliation? Jacob decides he will try and smooth his way in advance by sending gifts and flattering messages. Before long, Jacob has sent everyone traveling with him—his family, his servants, and all his livestock—ahead of him, and he's alone in the night. The Bible says that he wrestled there with a man—or in some translations, with an angel—until dawn.

I've had nights when I have wrestled with who I have been and who I am becoming. "Am I going to step forward into this new experience, or am I going to step back into the comfort of the familiar?" The biblical story says that Jacob wrestled with the angel until dawn, and as they wrestled, the angel touched Jacob in the hollow of his thigh and it was out of joint. Can you imagine wrestling with your thigh out of joint? Painful. My own late-night inner wrestling often has had emotional or mental pain involved in it.

But Jacob wouldn't let go of the angel, who finally said to him, "Let me go, it's almost daybreak." Jacob replied, "I won't let you go until you bless me!" The angel, impressed, said to him, "Who are you, what's your name?" Jacob said, "I am Jacob." But the angel replied, "Oh, no, not anymore you're not. Your name is now Israel, because you have power with God and man, and you have prevailed."

In everyday terms, Jacob had persisted in the inner struggle until he had fully evolved into what he was becoming. The angel represents what we are evolving into, while the wrestling represents both our desire to grow into that new identity and our resistance to leaving behind that which is familiar. When we do the wrestling without giving up in resignation to what has always been, we become a new person. When we are transformed into something new, we have a new identity, and in Jacob's case, a new name.

When I was hired by my first church as a new minister, I was not finished with the change process that began with the traumatic event of my divorce. I was entering the transformative part of that process that was set into motion by my choice of action following the grieving, awareness, and willingness. I might have chosen not to pursue the ministry at all, but to keep my minimum-wage job, stay in my hometown, feeling stuck. I might have chosen to fight with my former husband over property or custody rights. These choices would have had their own challenges, but they could have kept me rooted in the past had I wanted a reason to hang on. I wanted to go forward, and in making that choice I had to wrestle with the fears of the unknown that came from choosing newness in my life.

A dear friend from Seattle drove to northern California with me and stayed for the first week. I remember saying good-bye to her and watching the airport bus pull out of the parking lot. As it drove away I remember thinking to myself, "What have I done? I have no idea how to do this. I know no one here. I'm miles from my home, my son, my family. I must be out of my mind!" And I went into the park next door and cried.

When we are in the process of wrestling, our willingness may begin to fade, and we sometimes think, "Oh, I give up. That's it. I can't do it!" We may give up our emerging good, like the character in the play I saw, because we think we have so much difficulty to overcome. Even a temporary giving up isn't really the end in life, though. When we've rested we may find ourselves wrestling again. The tendency within us to grow is usually stronger than our resistance and fear of the unknown. It doesn't go away easily. Edison supposedly tried ten thousand times before he made a lightbulb that worked. It is said that someone asked him, "How does it feel, failing to prove your idea?" He was totally baffled. He responded,

"What do you mean? I have *successfully eliminated* over nine thousand ways to make a lightbulb!" If someone we know today tackled something with that kind of persistence, we'd sign him up for a twelve-step group. We'd say, "Tom, this is an addiction. Let it go! It's not working!" But there is no limit on the number of tries we may take in the transformative wrestling match between the I-was and the I-am-becoming.

I had to enter into the kind of inner struggle that pits the identity of the past against the emerging identity of the future. In that struggle I encountered fear, doubt, confusion, a feeling of inadequacy, inexperience, and loneliness. I wanted to give up and run home, but thankfully, I didn't. I stayed and struggled with the newness—in my work, my role, my personal sense of identity—and in doing so I discovered capacities I'd hoped I had. I watched and felt myself in my new role as minister. I found compassion, fairness, the ability to listen and to handle difficult people and situations, all growing stronger day by day. I made mistakes, but in the process I found a self I had never known, and one I believe I might never have found had I made the choice to hold on to the past.

Each time we come to a transitional place in our lives, this sequence of unfoldments is set into motion once more. This is true for us collectively and globally, too. A spiritual colleague of mine who began his career as a mathematician once said, "I used to believe that all scientific discoveries took place in an orderly sequence, each one building upon the one that went before. But when I researched them I found that this wasn't true at all. What actually happened was that as each new discovery emerged it completely blew the previous paradigm asunder!"

Personally and collectively, change is part of our nature, whether we welcome it or not. Understanding and cooperating with this sequence of unfoldments as the healthy, natural activity of the Divine Feminine in our lives can be the key to allowing the change to take us into transformation, revealing wondrous parts of ourselves that were hitherto unknown. The sequence of unfoldments that begins as grief can end in glory.

Action that transforms us grows out of the parts of our life that came before. It grows out of the grieving. It grows out of the looking up, becoming aware, discovering our willingness to act. The validity of that action is tested and proven by the struggle that follows it. The mystical alchemy of awareness, willingness, positive action, and struggle results in the revelation of a new being.

When we have successfully wrestled with the angel, our sense of identity shifts. Not only that but our interpretation of the momentous event that started our grieving can also shift. Initially our tendency is to view painful experiences as loss and limitation. We see wholeness as having things restored to the way they previously were. When we come through the inner struggle, we often have a new perspective on the catalytic event itself. We see how the devastation of the initial event led to the sequence of unfoldments that followed it, and the choices we made in each of those unfoldments contributed to the goodness of life now. We can sometimes see, in retrospect, that the initial event held the seeds of blessing all the time.

Although I was already in the school of ministry and planning a new career when my divorce took place, I believe I have more compassion because of the pain I experienced in the divorce. Yes, I would have learned new things and gained new strengths naturally in entering a new field, but I experienced these in an accelerated way because I entered this new life alone. I had to learn quickly to cope with everything that came my way. My faith was deepened, because I had God first and foremost to rely on for support and guidance in decisions I had to make. I felt God, manifesting as the Divine Feminine within and around me, much more strongly in my life than ever before. While it seemed a devastating loss and limitation in my life when it occurred, my divorce and the events that led up to it could be seen as important clues. In retrospect, they became bits of information that pointed the way to a vital message for me, saying, "The next steps in your life, you must take on your own."

When we are in grief because something is lost in our experience, we keenly feel the limitation. We feel the hole where that something precious once was. When we come to the point where we've completed the transformational struggle, we may instead see that the loss was not limitation but information from which to build a new life.

Not everyone chooses to come that far. Some may choose to

stay with the interpretation of limitation. Mark Twain wrote that a cat, once it has sat on a hot stove, will never do so again, but neither will it sit on a cold stove. So the cat permanently loses an opportunity because it has made too big a generalization. Human beings have the opportunity to make big generalizations, but they also have the opportunity to distinguish between hot and cold stoves. A divorce can stimulate one person to disavow personal relationships permanently. It can teach another how to grow so that her next relationship is more successful, and she is stronger and more compassionate.

In addition to the personal, there are communal and global instances in which reinterpreting ideas of limitation can reveal them as information. When this is done, those limited ideas need no longer stop us from going forward into the newness we feel called to express.

Author, motivator, and dynamo Tony Robbins says that his life was once as unsuccessful as it is abundantly good today. He was jobless and overweight, his girlfriend had just broken up with him, and his apartment was so small he had to wash the dishes in his bathtub. In an attempt to unravel the mystery of success, Tony began to observe successful people he admired. His theory was that if he could identify what they were doing that was effective and repeat what they had done, he could achieve similar results. It took time, and there were numerous, difficult setbacks, but in the long run it worked for him, both professionally and personally. To accomplish this goal, he had to stop seeing his past failures as reasons to be self-critical and begin to look at them as valuable experience from which to make better decisions. He had discovered some of what *didn't* work—that was valuable information. Now it was time to find out what *did* work.

Today Tony's students number in the thousands worldwide, and many of them are well-known personalities who swear by his techniques. He has even worked with the military to improve the performance of their sharpshooters, although he knew nothing about the skill. How? First, Tony asked and received permission to observe their finest sharpshooters. He watched them carefully, asked questions, and compiled all of the information. Tony assembled the finest knowledge and performance of the most talented shooters and taught those techniques to all the students, whose performance improved dramatically. Tony never fired a shot.

What if he had become discouraged by all of the obstacles he had to overcome to reach his goals? What if Tony had quit trying? Lots of people might still be struggling to find out why their personal and professional efforts weren't bringing about the desired results. Tony chose to look for the information that would turn his failures into successes. He committed himself to a personal vision of a better life and then expanded that vision to include better lives for others. As a result, many people are happier and more successful today than they were before they heard of Tony Robbins.

We have that same possibility within us, at least at the level of changing our own lives. If we are aware that it is time to take action and have both willingness and resistance to doing so, we will find ourselves wrestling at the urging of the Divine Feminine—that inner urgency to change and grow that keeps demanding our attention. The wrestling process can transform our self-image, our viewpoint about our current circumstances, and the actions that we take when the struggle is done.

It has wisely been said, "Change your thinking, change your life," but a person can be very skilled at pretending to change his thinking, even convincing himself. We see this in folks who have all the right information, and can repeat it easily, but never seem to apply it actively to their lives. Somehow we don't buy it that they really believe what they are professing, because their lives show no evidence of being lived from that knowledge or belief. What is the evidence that one's thinking has truly changed? The evidence is that one's behavior changes. If our thinking has truly changed, the action we take in our lives growing out of that thinking will also change. If we are all talk and no action, we have not embraced and embodied the new information with which we have become intellectually familiar. We are still responding in the same old ways, which will continue to produce the same old results. If our behavior doesn't change, our thinking hasn't changed.

A member of my church once gave me a cartoon of a fellow sitting in an arm chair in front of the television. As he's sitting there, the fellow is saying to himself, "Yep, I'm getting up now, here I go. Upsy-daisy. That's me getting up." But he never moves. And the caption underneath the cartoon says, "The power of positive thinking is no match for the power of negative doing." It's the truth, isn't it? The power of positive thinking is no match for the power of negative doing. Whether we *act* upon our thinking or not determines the results we experience. If our thinking and our belief have been changed, the way in which we respond will also change. Repeating positive ideas won't change our lives unless our action is in alignment with those ideas. Of course, this is much easier to discuss than it is to do.

Many of us think we want to be transformed, but we don't want to be inconvenienced. In the change process, however, we *are* inconvenienced. How many of us would like improvements in our lives but do not want those improvements to affect us in any uncomfortable way? We want to be wealthy without the responsibilities that come with wealth. We want to be healthy without exercise, good diet, or practices for dealing with stress. We want the perfect mate, but we want to be loved unconditionally, with no expectations from the other person for growth on our part. How realistic are these desires? To improve our lives in any way is to step into an unfamiliar territory. That is usually uncomfortable. The difficult event that catapults us into the sequence of unfoldments can help us move toward those improvements we've always said we want by changing more than the important outer circumstances of our lives. That event of loss opens the way to changing *us* at a deep level. Inconvenient, yes, but it is amazingly transformational.

Leaving behind grief, which is familiar, and entering into awareness can be scary. A new choice could prove to be a poor one. Wrestling can be painful, and action comes with no guarantee of success. Why do any of us bother following the sequence of unfoldments through to completion after the event of loss? We bother because the choice to stay the same is painful, costly, and, in the long run, more difficult than going with the change process as it unfolds.

A longtime friend and I spent our younger years supporting each other through all sorts of difficult relationships. We did so out of love, because we often couldn't understand the other's choice of partner. But both of us were committed to a path of growth and self-actualization. Eventually we both found the partners of our hearts' longing after many attempts to become better partners ourselves and to choose wisely. These attempts sometimes brought more sense of loss, but after a time, we both experienced increased success after applying what we had learned from previous relationships. The journey was arduous, but the outcome was worth it.

John, another friend, chose to stay in a long-term marriage that was verbally and emotionally abusive. Crises would occur. Opportunities to make changes in himself or the situation were passed over again and again. Instead he complained about how he was treated, and pursued love affairs with other women. He would overeat or stay extremely busy to avoid the discomfort of his life. His health was precarious; his self-esteem was low. His children emulated their mother, speaking to him cruelly and treating him without respect. He took it all with scarcely a word of discipline or reproof. Suggestions from his friends were met with objections and evidence of why they couldn't possibly work. The cost of maintaining the status quo was energetically, emotionally, and physically expensive to him, yet he was unwilling to choose to move forward.

We are designed to grow and adapt, and when we choose not to do so, life can be very difficult. There is a cost involved in resisting our own personal, natural evolution. Each one of us has a brilliant magnificence within that pushes to be revealed. Resisting that push prevents us from discovering the potential within us. It keeps some of the gifts within us hidden from our sight and robs the world of the potential contribution those gifts might make.

In Bangkok, Thailand, there is a shrine called the Temple of the Golden Buddha. It looks small from the outside, but inside there is a stunning ten-and-a-half-foot-tall golden Buddha. It weighs more than two and a half tons and is valued at $195 million.

But the statue wasn't always recognized for what it is. In 1957, a group of monks from a nearby local monastery had to relocate their temple, and along with it a large clay Buddha, because of renovations going on in their city. So they hoisted the statue up into the air, but as they lifted it, two things happened. The clay on the Buddha began to crack, and rain began to fall.

The monk in charge of the process became concerned that

the statue might be damaged, so he lowered it and covered it with tarps. The rain went on, as the rain can do in Thailand, and the monk went out in the middle of the night to check on the Buddha and see how it was faring. As he shone his flashlight under the tarp, a gleam came back at him, and he thought, *That's odd. What is that?* He decided to lift the tarp and examine the gleam. He saw gold beneath the clay and began to chip away at the layers of earth. As it fell away, more and more gold was revealed, until, many hours later, the monks were confronted with an immense, solid-gold Buddha.

Apparently several centuries earlier during one of the Burmese invasions of the country, then called Siam, the Siamese monks in the monastery that owned the gold Buddha had covered it with eight inches of clay to prevent the Burmese from desecrating or stealing it. Unfortunately, all of those Siamese monks were killed in the invasion, so nobody survived who knew the secret. It wasn't until 1957 that the gold inside was revealed and the story pieced together.

And so it is with us. In our process of change, we, too, get jostled around and cracked. That transformative process is like taking a hammer and chisel to the old self and revealing what is underneath the surface. What is within is the golden Buddha. A treasure of shining magnificence and divine wisdom, the Infinite Creative Presence, exists in every one of us.

There is another reason we may choose the path of unfoldments that follows a life-changing event. Once we embark on it, we can discover that this way of responding to change —

through grief, awareness, willingness, action, and struggle —
is healing and life affirming. The moving, living energy of the
Divine Feminine within us urges us forward, entices us into
our potential. We can always choose to avoid this path of
growth and to attempt to keep things as much like the past as
possible even after the shock occurs, but this choice is costly.
Everything living continues to change and grow. To resist this
internal wisdom is to swim upstream against our own nature.
This is what makes the difficult unfoldments that can follow a
life-shattering moment worth taking. This is why many of us
do go forward — because something about these unfoldments
is irresistible. That golden Buddha within waits to be revealed
to us and to the world. The blessing of the darkness we call
change is that it opens the door to transformation if we allow
it to become a blessing rather than a curse. Every one of us
brings unique gifts, unique treasures to the world, but without a willingness to grow, we may never discover them.
It is the role of the Divine Feminine within us to urge us
toward the unfoldments, motivate us to cooperate with them,
and guide us, through our own natural intuitiveness, successfully through them into a fuller expression of ourselves.

Two

The Gift of Fear, and the Courage to Enter the Darkness

....

The next time you encounter fear, consider yourself lucky. This is where the courage comes in. Usually we think that brave people have no fear. The truth is that they are intimate with fear. When I was first married, my husband said I was one of the bravest people he knew. When I asked him why, he said because I was a complete coward but went ahead and did things anyhow.

—*Pema Chödrön,* When Things Fall Apart: Heart Advice for Difficult Times

In the film *The Empire Strikes Back,* Luke Skywalker is being trained by Jedi master teacher Yoda when they come upon a deep underground cave on Yoda's planet. "There's something not right here," Luke says. "I feel cold. Death." Yoda tells Luke, "That place—is strong with the Dark Side of the Force. A domain of evil it is. In you must go."

"What's in there?" Luke asks. "Only what you take with

you" is the reply. As Luke begins to strap on his light saber, Yoda shakes his head saying, "Your weapons—you will not need them." But Luke, giving him a look of skepticism, disregards the instruction and takes the weapon anyway.

What do we take with us when we go into battle with "evil" or what we perceive as a threat? Do we fail to listen to the wisdom of our mentors, the "masters" around us, as Luke did, out of fear and the belief that our ability to attack will save us? Do we run away and hide? Or do we find ourselves unable to act at all when confronted with something we fear or dread?

Fear is one of the greatest challenges facing us today. Perhaps we fear loss of a partner, or rejection by a family or group, because of their anger or disapproval. We may experience fear of pain or poverty, loneliness or death. We may fear being shamed, criticized, or abandoned. Those who fear abuse may lose themselves trying to please the abuser or attempting to become invisible to prevent further pain. We fear losing what we already have or losing the hope of improving what we have. And these fears aren't limited to individuals. Neighborhoods, businesses, countries, and continents have fears that are the sum total of the fears of their inhabitants. We are facing a global epidemic of fear, which can often appear under the guise of righteous anger or pragmatic realism. Fear of takeover or attack by other countries continues to perpetuate the possibility of war and terrorism. Fear of being lied to by governments causes outlandish suspicions, dangerous preparations for violence, and actions of vengeance for imagined wrongs. Fear of powerlessness to improve one's life causes crime, drug abuse, and violence all over the world. From this perspective, fear is truly an experience of the darkness, something to be avoided at all costs.

This fear of loss and lack reduces humankind's ability individually and collectively to express and experience the fullness of creation and our place in it. How can an individual express his magnificent potential while preparing to fight or flee? His energy and creativity are too busy with defense to be available for deeper development. How can a nation or a planet thrive when its inhabitants are immersed in their fears? Albert Einstein once made the statement that it is impossible to simultaneously prepare for war and move toward peace. This insight summarizes the challenge of fear. We feel it and we don't like it. We want to feel truly safe. How then to respond to fear appropriately, creating its opposite, peacefulness, rather than increased fear?

No one claims fear is a pleasant experience. Our fear is experienced as some degree of suffering. We do all we can to relieve ourselves of the feeling as soon as possible by whatever means we think will be most effective. Some of us hide, some attack, others eat, still others become angry or apathetic and depressed. We use distractions to forget the fear, or aggression to combat its supposed source.

Occasionally the energy of the fear motivates us to examine and question the fear itself. Here, then, is a key to the way out of the maze of fear. What if fear has another purpose than motivating us to fight or flee?

Fear is a pervasive human experience, and a powerful one. Typically it either paralyzes us or motivates us to action. When it paralyzes us, life goes on hold—we become stuck. When it motivates us, it may do so positively or negatively. Negative motivation leads to defensive actions that assume the "other" will take something from us unless we attack. When it motivates us positively, we respond by taking action that is informed by a view larger than just our personal interests. It includes ourselves, the situation, and the other persons involved in it from a win-win perspective. This action can often both benefit everyone involved and improve the situation itself.

The result of holding on to fear and letting it direct our actions is that it perpetuates more fear. It makes the fear seem justified, reinforcing its existence. It also evokes a corresponding fear in others, both our "allies" and our "enemies." Our enemy's fear (usually masked as anger) seems to him to justify a retaliatory attack. The problem escalates rather than being resolved. This is reflected, on a large scale, in gang warfare and, on a personal scale, in communication problems in our relationships.

But what if the purpose of fear is something more transformative than creating paralysis, attack, or retreat? What if fear comes bearing gifts to increase our courage, awareness, and resiliency? And how can we access these gifts? Not through the familiar methods of attacking, running away, or becoming paralyzed. Our old methods of coping with fear are part of what sustains our interpretations of fear's meaning.

In many cases, both our methods of coping with fear and our interpretation of it need examining. This approach is typical of responding to fear with the Guidance of the Divine Feminine: instead of choosing to fight, flee, or surrender to paralysis, we look at the fear itself, trusting that there is a message in the fear experience that can lead us forward to greater harmony.

When Luke Skywalker descends deep into the cave, he unknowingly goes into the darkest part of himself. He discovers his greatest fear there, his enemy, Darth Vader, and he draws his light saber to defend himself, engaging the dark warrior in battle. Luke defeats Vader and cuts off his head, only to discover that behind Vader's mask is Luke's very own face. Like Luke, all of us must go within to face the darkness there. This inner darkness is a greater unknown than any external threat, and for many of us it is *this* darkness that causes most of our fear, not the external circumstances, however compelling they may seem.

Luke tried, as some of us do from time to time, to fight fear as if it were an outsider, with anger and violence and resistance. But the darkness of Luke's fear, as with most of us, begins within. It becomes negative when we repress and resist it. The Divine Feminine—that aspect of ourselves that always moves toward balance—brings fear to our awareness so that we may realize we are facing a feeling of limitation: we don't know what to do about the fear. We need Guidance and information in order to respond appropriately to fear.

When we see fear as a messenger meant to stimulate a new response, we become more resilient and innovative in seeking that response. But when we instead deny and avoid fear, it becomes an enemy, pursuing us relentlessly, and becoming larger and larger until we face it and find out its message. When we allow fear to motivate us to negative action, regardless of any other outcomes, it is always ourselves we hurt. Defensive actions teach us to be *more* afraid rather than less. Such actions weaken our resilience as we expend our precious energy for defense or attack. Fear shuts down our creativity. Life becomes smaller.

A dear friend of mine who used to help me with dream interpretation noticed that every time I brought a dream to her in which I had felt fear and great upset, the underlying message was actually positive. Usually in these dreams I ran, or in some other way avoided, that which was pursuing me. "Why don't you turn and ask that dark figure what she wants?" Carleita would say, or, "Have you tried imaging yourself as the pursuer you see in the dream? If you become the pursuer, what is it you want?" When I reentered the dream while awake and tried those things, inevitably the message from the pursuer was not only pertinent but essential for that moment in my life. But had I continued to view the pursuer I feared as negative, I never would have received the message.

Carleita was giving me a lesson in opening to the Divine Feminine. Rather than interpreting the dream at face value, I learned to look deeper within myself for more helpful information about the dream, with the assumption that such information was indeed there. In looking at the dream with the assumption of benefit, I did discover meanings that were hidden when I only looked at it literally. This technique of allowing deeper information to reveal itself from the substance of our dreams is one way of receiving Guidance from the Divine Feminine.

Waking life is not so different from dreams. Aside from fear that genuinely warns us to fight or flee in order to protect our lives, most fear is a friend come to give an important message: we have work to do in some area of our life in order to grow into greater freedom. Facing our fear *in that specific situation* can provide the needed work and growth. The message and messengers continue to show up until we do the work and taste the freedom.

Surveys show that fear of speaking in public is the number-one fear in America. Death is number two or three. This means most people would rather die than speak in public. As a drama major in college, I had the opportunity to feel that fear. I was the understudy for the lead role in a three-hour university production of Bertolt Brecht's *The Good Person (Woman) of Setzuan,* a role in which the actor must play two parts: the kindhearted Shen Te and her fictitious, hard-nosed businessman cousin, Shui Ta. No one with a lead that juicy ever misses a performance. The position of understudy was a compliment, but one with no expectation of performance. Nothing was required of me. I was never rehearsed in the role. No one ever checked to see if I knew the lines or the blocking for the part. I continued to play the small, supporting role in which I had also been cast with no thought that one night I might have my chance to play the lead—that is, until 11:00 P.M. on St. Patrick's Day, when I returned home from an evening of Irish celebration and received a phone call from the play's director.

"How well do you know the role of Shen Te?" he asked me. "Why do you want to know?" I replied. "Because Anne isn't feeling well, and she thinks if she performs tomorrow night she may not make it through the rest of the week. I want to know if you can do it." "You bet I can!" I answered him. I was enthused at the opportunity. At the same time, I was frightened out of my wits. What if I forgot my lines, or one of the songs? What if I messed up a costume change? What if I froze altogether? I had never had this kind of demand placed on my abilities before, and I really didn't know what might happen under such pressure. All I knew was, in spite of the fear, I wanted more than anything to try.

I didn't sleep much that night, and the next day I cut all my classes and met with the rest of the cast in shifts to go over my scenes with them at the campus theater where we performed the play each night. In reality, I found I knew most of the lines for the part. As I was just offstage for most of the play, I had listened and watched over and over again as Anne performed the role during our run. With the exception of two scenes during which I was usually in the dressing room, I had absorbed the lines without ever specifically memorizing them. And now, in my rushed rehearsals, there were places in those two scenes where I inevitably seemed to "go up" and lose all sense of what came next.

We pressed on with rehearsals toward zero hour. Someone brought me meals. I never once left the building before the evening call, the time all performers are due in their dressing rooms.

Our set was a large, surrealistic one-piece design. It moved by means of a revolving floor in order to change the location of various scenes. There were openings in the set that served as doorways, a trapdoor, multiple levels, and a bridge over the orchestra pit on which scenes were played. Numerous costume changes (which were accomplished in blackout), in addition to my dual character, complicated the performance of the lead role.

That evening, as I stood on the top level of the set, just out of the audience's sight, with my back to the windowed wall flat I would soon look through to deliver my opening lines, I took deep breaths and repeated to myself over and over again, "I will not pass out. I will not pass out."

The cast was a tremendous support. During the brief blackouts they pushed me into position for my next scene (I was in all of them) and quickly pulled off my clothes and put on new ones as costume changes demanded. Sometimes I had no idea which scene was next until the lights came up on the set. And twice during the long performance, I did forget my lines — during the two scenes that occurred when I had been in the dressing room for so many performances.

We got through the performance reasonably well. All my friends from the drama department had come that night to cheer me on, and when I came down into the green room after the curtain call, the entire cast gave me a standing ovation. I burst into tears.

I had been terrified. Throughout the day I had periodically wondered if I'd lost my mind saying yes to this performance with no previous rehearsals. But what I found out was that I could perform under pressure and do a good job. I also discovered that fear and nervousness, in and of themselves, couldn't stop me. As long as I went on to do what I was there to do, these feelings had no power to prevent me from doing what I had dreamed of. Fear let me know that what was at stake meant a lot to me. It let me know I was in unfamiliar territory. Was my destiny to freeze, flee, fight with the cast, or follow the path through the fear? I didn't know until I chose to walk through the heart-pounding, palm-sweating fear and to do the performance.

Successfully performing in the midst of fear and unfamiliarity was one of the greatest lessons of my life, and one I still think of often. It continues to remind me that my fear cannot harm me. I can feel fearful and still be strong and effective. That is a powerful thing to know: when we are motivated to examine our inner fear, we go to the real source of the majority of our fears where we can best affect these feelings and bring about personal freedom.

When we choose to confront our fear, we can move through it and, in doing so, discover its hidden gifts. In making this choice, we become free of the imprisoning nature of the fear. We let go of what we are tightly clinging to. Now a whole range of responses may become visible. We may more easily see the results of fear working in both our allies and our enemies and make choices for ourselves based upon the results we want to achieve rather than simply preserving what we're afraid to lose. Fear overcome is transformed into greater freedom and peacefulness. As a bonus, facing our fear reveals courage and ingenuity we often did not realize we possessed.

When the Divine Feminine reveals one of our fears to us and we become acutely aware of it, our first defense against the feeling is often attack or denial (a form of hiding or fleeing). It is the *next* choice of response we make, after the first automatic one, that is critical to the results we produce. It is possible to continue to do what we're doing *while feeling the fear* without continuing to resort to our usual defenses. If we do this, we are consciously allowing the Divine Feminine to lead the way in unfamiliar territory.

If we want the freedom to fulfill our life's purpose with creativity and joy, we must eventually identify fear's voice. When we understand its purpose and code, we see that the voice is not a call to arms. Nor is it a stoplight to prevent us from going forward. More often, fear signals a transition in progress. It lets us know something important is at risk. It wakes us up to the awareness that some action is required. In most cases, that action is to move through the fear itself, not letting it stop us from moving toward our goal, and not attacking others thinking they can prevent our good. We move through the fear by relaxing, taking the smallest possible baby steps in the direction of our goal, and taking the time to assess if there *really* is any threat from another. Most of the time our feeling of fear is so much larger than any real danger. The only way we find out for sure is to put our courage on the line and walk directly into what we fear. The courageous soul isn't one who feels no fear but one who acts in spite of it.

What happens when we choose avoidance of the thing we fear rather than taking hold of it head-on? We never discover that its apparent power is an illusion. What we fear continues to seem real, and we remain bound in its grasp. Several years ago, a friend of mine found herself in this position. Toni made good money at her job but was bored with it. Her hobby was art, and she enjoyed it so much she decided to go to school to study it and move toward it as her livelihood. She had been accepted at a good school and had paid the admission and first term of tuition when fear took over. "Look how much this is going to cost! What if I go and find out I'm not good at this after all? What if I leave my job and spend these years and all this money and when I finish I'm no happier than I am now?" She canceled her registration and asked for a refund.

Toni became paralyzed by her own fear. Fear that she

would not have enough money. Fear that she would be less, rather than more, happy. Instead of following and trusting her inner Guidance toward a more fulfilling life, she followed her fear, and it limited her life and expression. Schooling may not have guaranteed Toni the life she wanted, but she would have learned that *following your heart is the path that takes you gradually to the next step you need in your life*. Toni's plan, had she followed it, would have placed her in a new environment with new people, new contacts, and new experiences. Perhaps she wouldn't have become a professional artist, but moving along the path that called to her would have opened up possibilities leading to a life she couldn't imagine from where she was: a life she couldn't create for herself without the learning she would gain from the new experiences life was offering. Fear signaled to her that this was a major change of tremendous importance. But rather than recognizing it as a code for transition, she interpreted the fear as a danger signal and let it stop her cold.

The good news is that although Toni passed up that opportunity, there will be more. They will continue to come until she decides to go forward in spite of her fear, and when she does so, her fear will be diminished and her joy increased, no matter what the outcome. She will be more free. From there, she will be more able to accept the fulfilling life she wants. Choosing to stay with the known prevents us from entering the realm of magic that is the Divine Feminine: the realm of undiscovered possibilities.

But we will be called there again. Again and again, we are urged to fulfill our potential. The Divine Feminine never gives up on us. It provides us with as many opportunities as we need to face our fears and learn from them.

A dear friend of mine, Rev. Karyl Huntley, gives the example of baby penguins learning to swim. As Karyl tells it, when it's time for the babies to learn, their parents take them out to the edge of the ice floe. The parents jump into the icy water and call to the babies from below. Some babies immediately jump into the water and begin to swim. Others pace the edge, calling back and forth to the parents. Eventually they, too, jump, or slip and fall, into the water and begin swimming. The last group of penguins can never get up the courage to jump in. They remain on the floe calling to the parents. Eventually the tide comes in and sweeps the remaining babies off the ice floe and into the water, where they also begin swimming. None is left behind. Every one of them inherently has the power to swim, but each one must, in one way or another, get into the water to discover it. Likewise, each one of us has the power to walk through our inner fears, but we must wade out into them to experience the power.

A perceived sense of loss underlies most of our fears. We wish to avoid the experience we *think* we will have if we lose that money, approval, job, relationship, health, or security. On some level we feel we could not survive if we lost *that*. But the Divine Feminine means to show us that we are bigger than any fear. In some cases, we must lose it all in order to let the fear go. When we have nothing left to lose, we often discover we can do what we thought we could not.

Carl was a man I knew with a serious alcohol problem. He wanted it to go away through prayer so he could drink socially and not have to change anything in his life. His reason for avoiding Alcoholics Anonymous was that as a highly visible member of our community, he might encounter clients at local meetings and this, he felt, would damage his trustworthiness and authority in their eyes. He resented being encouraged to meet with others in recovery. "Yes, I've talked to him," he'd say dismissively. "He's a 'grateful' former drunk." Over the course of his struggles Carl lost his family, his job, and his home, and made several attempts to end his life. He entered and left a number of detox programs before they had a chance to really work.

We saw each other after one of his attempts to commit suicide. He was drunk, sick, and miserable. Quietly he shed tears of shame, and spoke of wanting to die. He knew there were options available for help but was unwilling to take them. I told him gently that, in essence, what he was telling me was that he'd rather die than change. I felt nothing that I said was getting through, and when he left it seemed to me I might never see Carl alive again.

Later that evening I called a fellow minister and two other friends who were recovering alcoholics and asked if there was anything I'd missed. What else could I have said or done? Each responded that there was nothing to do but to let Carl go, and if he killed himself it was not my fault. It was up to him. That was hard to hear. I thanked each one and tried to follow their suggestions, enfolding Carl and myself in prayer and releasing him to Spirit.

Almost the next thing I knew, Carl was genuinely in recovery, and this time it seemed to be for himself rather than for the sake of preserving his job or his family. He could no longer bargain for those things, since there was no one left to try to convince or urge to get off his back. He had made the internal shift on his own, finally knowing he couldn't live as he'd been doing anymore. Carl took one day at a time to do what he could, with support, to stop drinking and save his own life.

Detox and recovery hospitals had not worked for him before. Numerous times he'd walked out, going back to the addiction that was slowly ending his life. This time was different. Why? Carl was finally ripe for the choice, having lost everything he feared losing. In the twelve-step terms of Alcoholics Anonymous, he had hit bottom, and it hadn't killed him. The Divine Feminine had revealed a mystery: Carl could lose it all and not die. Carl's response to his fear of loss had begun as a negative one that nearly killed him, but it ended with a courageous choice for life and freedom.

From that time on, his life improved. He recovered his health, he won back his job, and he found a new home and relationship. More important, he recovered his sense of self-worth. The crisis of choice in that darkness of despair and self-hatred meant leaping into the unknown and doing what seemed to him most frightening and difficult. Carl made that choice, and following it with small, steady, sequential steps transformed his life. But it took losing everything that mattered to Carl to push him into his fear until it shattered. That shattering opened the door that led back to wholeness. His fear had grown through his avoidance of it, until it became his life. But he chose to take a path *through* it, and that choice made him strong. Fear had finally motivated him to positive action, and in that action he found freedom.

The Divine Feminine is that within us that nudges us to face fear and trust the outcome to Spirit. As we do so, the Divine Feminine reveals increased courage, strength, and deepened integrity in our daily lives. Integrity is defined as that which is whole and undivided. In human beings I see it as the pure undiluted power of honesty and truth. That quality is easily visible in small children but is diminished as we grow up in our efforts to please others and see to it that we get what we want. We speak the truth less clearly, not only to others but ultimately to ourselves as well. When we are able to admit and enter into our fears, then walk through them to safety, integrity begins to be restored. When that happens, we become stronger, freer people.

Courage, strength, resilience, ingenuity, and integrity: these, then, are the gifts that fear itself brings to us if we face it rather than freezing, fleeing, or fighting. It takes courage to walk into the darkness and through that fire, but our personal fears, both large and small, are what we all must face. No one can stand in for us, nor can we successfully do so for someone else. Uniquely suited to each of us, the path ahead provides all the choices and challenges necessary for the fullest unfoldment of the Divine within.

Each time we choose to face our fear, our self-esteem and our personal power are increased by choosing to trust the Guidance of the Divine Feminine. While we may feel paralyzed, like Toni, or motivated to negative action, like Luke Skywalker, we may finally find that the most empowering choice is the one I stumbled upon, and which Carl came to after long struggles with his fear. When we confront fear, and walk through it to freedom, we experience the transformative power of the Divine Feminine. We discover that our fears are mostly illusion and that there is more resilience and strength within us than we knew. We receive a great gift of freedom: the gift of knowing that fear can never again prevent us from moving through the unknown and pursuing our dreams.

Three

Anger: Friend or Enemy?

....

Stitch up my heart with golden thread.
May a new strength grow in the broken places.
Give me the courage to feel the pain of betrayal
and the compassion to let it go.
Teach me to forgive myself as I struggle to forgive others.
And where there are no answers,
may the questions become a prayer.

—*Science of Mind student*

Of all the strong emotions we experience, anger is perhaps the one we struggle with the most. Despite the recognition that anger is a necessary and healthy emotion, put forward by modern psychology in numerous self-help books, and the emergence of anger workshops to help people feel the emotion and find their way to appropriate expressions of it, anger still tends to be viewed by many of us as dark, dangerous, and negative. While we continue to make efforts toward transforming our approach to anger, it is clear that as a culture, we have not yet grasped this emotion's healing potential. The evening news is filled with stories of anger gone awry: abuse of children, spouses, and elders; gang violence; rape; and murder. We seem to see anger most often connected to the effects of poverty, injustice, lack of education and opportunity, drug and alcohol abuse, and stress.

In spite of all this darkness, could it be that there really is a positive side to anger? Is it possible that anger is an emotion that can have a constructive purpose? Could it be that anger can reveal important passages to personal awareness and power and thereby lead us to greater wholeness?

The answer is yes. When the Divine Feminine reveals Itself in us in the form of anger, It invites us to *look into the anger itself.* By doing this rather than blaming an outside provocateur for our feelings, we see that our anger has gifts for us, which, as we discovered in our exploration of fear, reveal themselves when we face the emotion rather than denying it or blaming it on others. When we take responsibility for our anger and look for its source within ourselves, we can harvest long-term benefits.

In indigenous religious traditions, among myriad gods and goddesses we often see the face of anger as well as the faces of love, justice, wisdom, and compassion. At its root, the Hindu faith honors a divine trinity: Brahma, the Creator; Vishnu, the Sustainer; and Shiva, the Destroyer. Fierce but far from being evil, the god Shiva destroys whatever has served its purpose and is no longer useful. That which is destroyed becomes the compost from which newness comes, releasing energy formerly bound up in the old to be used in the creation of the new.

In Hindu lore, one of the holy faces of anger is the face of the goddess Kali. Consort to Shiva, Kali is one of the feminine faces of the destroyer. She represents the fierce warrior aspect of the Divine Feminine. As Merlin Stone wrote in *Ancient Mirrors of Womanhood,*

> Kali is the essence of Night . . . dancer of the cremation ground . . . surrounded by wailing female spirits, a garland of heads about Her neck, a belt of human hands about Her waist, blood upon Her lips . . . Daughter of the Ocean, Mother born of Anger . . . they say that death lingers in the waters of Her womb. . . .

One of Kali's powers is the destruction of human ignorance. She is sometimes portrayed wearing a necklace of skulls, carrying a skull bowl in one hand and a machete in the other. An ancient story tells us that in Kali's bowl, our ego self is chopped and chopped until our ignorance is exposed and destroyed and our true essence is revealed. Kali's anger has a purpose that is actually compassionate. Through her relentless attention to exactly what needs to be destroyed, she sets us free to be our fuller selves. Kali shows us that her anger *at our ignorance,* and the action she takes to destroy that ignorance, can become a vehicle for our healing and transformation.

In this, Kali is a model for behavior in response to anger that we might do well to emulate. As we look into the feeling of anger, we may discover its causes are ignorant attitudes that really aren't working in our lives. Exposing them, we can work to let them go and replace them with more productive attitudes, thereby healing ourselves.

Anger can also transform when we learn how to interpret and express it. In my life, and in my work as a minister, I see that repressed anger does great damage to the person resisting expressing that feeling. It can result in depression and physical illness. Yet the expression of anger that is allowed to rampantly trample all those around it is equally damaging. Releasing anger in an abusive way may temporarily take the pressure off the person feeling the emotion, but doing so without care can permanently damage lives and relationships.

As I examine my own history with anger, it seems to me that events over which I tend to become angry fall into three categories. One is the frustration that comes of not getting things my own way in situations in which I am highly attached to the outcome. In these instances, it is of utmost importance to me that a particular result come about. When it doesn't, I may feel a combination of emotions, and one of those may be anger. Once when I traveled out of state to participate in the family orientation program at my son's university, I missed my first flight due to confusion at the airport, which meant missing my connecting flight as well. Upon finally reaching my intermediate stop, I tried to rent a car to drive to my final destination, but every car in town had been rented for the weekend. Frustration over my lack of control of the circumstances made me increasingly angry. Even after alternative transportation to my destination was arranged, it took time to cool off.

A second category of event in which I tend to react with anger is one in which I am attached to a person whose action has hurt or disappointed me. I become upset because I believe the person involved should care about me in some way, yet his action seems out of alignment with that caring, which causes me pain or distress.

The third type of event in which I find myself responding with anger is one in which I am attached to a belief or principle so strongly that I am deeply offended by another's violation of it. Nationally we see such clashes occur frequently over people's differences of opinion regarding abortion, capital punishment, and the defense budget, among other issues.

In this discussion of anger and forgiveness I am primarily addressing the second and third categories of angry feelings — those that arise from relationships with other people, or conflicts over personal values, because these categories of anger are more likely to cause us ongoing pain. When we are attached to the outcome of an event that doesn't go our way, once the event itself has passed, we can often let the attachment go, too. We are then less likely to take the outcome of an event personally as we think about it over time. When I tried to visit my son, I was frustrated and angry at missing my flight and having no car, but when I think about it now, there's no residual upset left.

But let's consider what happens in our personal relationships. When people with whom we have a relationship are involved in an upsetting incident, we may be more likely to continue to think about the other person's behavior toward us and feel personally hurt by it. These hurts can replay themselves for years, usurping valuable energy in the remembering and ruminating that could be better used for building our lives *now*. In order to get past these hurts that continue to bother us, we need to learn how to forgive and let go. Learning how to forgive others is what this chapter's exploration of anger is all about. Therefore, let's first examine forgiveness in the context of personal relationships, and then we'll look at its application in situations of conflict over deeply held values.

We all have limits, or boundaries beyond which we don't want to be pushed, or that we don't want breached by others. Societies have identified boundaries that all members are expected to uphold. Personal and societal boundaries are necessary, as they identify the limits of behavior and personal interaction that are acceptable. Living in the world with other human beings means that sometimes we step on each other's toes. Boundary agreements help us to live together fairly and peacefully.

An example of a common individual boundary is personal

space. For some people, carrying on a conversation with another person only a few inches away is perfectly comfortable. For others, such closeness feels presumptuous and invasive.

Another boundary shows up around issues that are sensitive to a person or a family. Someone who does not want to discuss his brother's drinking or his daughter's overspending may react with anger when these subjects are broached.

A third boundary has to do with our perception of what is polite. If we feel it's inappropriate ever to say no to another person's request, we may feel angry when someone asks us to take on a task we don't want to do. Because we believe it is impolite to say no, we feel stuck, and may be resentful of the person making the request. "She knows I don't have time for this job! Why did she put me in the position to have to say yes? It's not fair of her to do that to me!" We may carry out the task resentfully, fail to do it at all, or do it poorly, all in an indirect attempt to communicate the no we felt but didn't say. This third boundary may also prevent us from asking people for what we want and need, as we project onto them our own inability to say no. We hesitate to breach the politeness boundary of others by asking for such things, even though we cannot know unless we ask, whether they have such a boundary! In not asking, we are attempting to read their minds, tending our imagined version of their boundaries for them. Likewise, we are expecting others to read our minds and tend our boundaries for us when we expect them to refrain from asking because we might want to say no.

The ways we protect our boundaries vary a great deal from one person to another. Some people actively express, both verbally and nonverbally, their displeasure when they feel a boundary is violated. Some folks are unaware of their own boundaries and don't readily know what they feel. They tend to make light of behavior others might find unacceptable. In some cases, they scarcely seem to notice abusive behavior at all. Still others know what they feel but are reluctant to express it, holding their discomfort inside and trying to mask their frustration toward the insensitivity of the boundary crosser in an attempt to be nice. Often in the latter two situations, the violated party lets out her pain or anger indirectly in a passive-aggressive manner. The classic example is the wife with hurt feelings who, in response to her husband's "Honey, what's wrong?" snarls, *"Nothing!"* and refuses to talk about it further, sulking until her husband is forced to guess what he's done to upset her. He has been manipulated—by the mismatch between her angry tone and her seemingly neutral choice of words—toward the response she wants from him.

My dear mother brought me up to believe that ladies were not to express anger directly. As a young teen, I remember trying to discuss something with her that I felt was reasonable, with which she clearly disagreed. She left the room in the middle of the conversation, went to the kitchen and began to fix dinner, banging cabinets and drawers and muttering to herself angrily. I soon learned there were things one doesn't discuss. I no longer remember the topic on which we disagreed, but I have never forgotten the outcome of trying to communicate about it.

Boundaries exist whether we tend to them actively or not, and whether they are realistic or not. Once a boundary is violated, there is an automatic, internal response of which most of us are aware. It is a flash of anger or frustration. Animals respond to each other immediately in such circumstances. My cats hiss and then swat when they feel invaded. My dog takes a lot, but will finally yip and snap at another dog when she has had enough.

Anger is our internal warning system that a boundary has been violated. It works like a smoke detector. Feeling angry makes us aware that we want, need, or expect something different from what we are getting, and that this is not all right with us. Anger points out that there is a gap between what we desire and the reality we are experiencing. It is an alarm that alerts us, saying "Appropriate action needs to be taken," either to restore the boundary or to examine it and see if it's time to replace it with something different. By making us aware that a need exists, anger opens the way for us to take responsibility for getting our needs met in a healthy way. But before we can move to that step, we must first recognize that we feel the emotion of anger and we must express it appropriately.

This is easier said than done. Many women have, like my mother, been brought up with the belief that it isn't ladylike to get angry. So rather than feel and express anger when it arises, we may feel guilty that we are angry, and try harder to be nice. Over time, we may lose touch with the feeling of anger altogether, finding ourselves depressed without knowing why. The suppression of feeling tends to build an internal stockpile of anger that can burst out all at once when the accumulation becomes too much to tolerate any longer. This kind of dumping usually baffles the recipient of our anger, who just sees that we are overreacting to the offense that set us off. Many men, in contrast, have often been taught not to be "sissies" but to stand up for themselves, not taking nonsense from anyone at any time. With this encouragement, it can be easier for men to feel their anger and express it, but this is no guarantee that the expression will be appropriate.

Our task is to recognize anger, find an appropriate expression of the emotion, and determine how to incorporate such expressions into our lives through practice. Once we have learned these things, we must learn to let go of our sense of being offended in order to finally heal. In order to recognize and feel anger, we must honor ourselves. In order to express the anger appropriately, we must honor our relationships with others. In order to let go of the hurt we must honor and trust that something larger is at work through the whole experience, bringing us good in spite of the pain. This flow from part to whole (focus moving from ourselves, to the other, to the whole situation) is characteristic of the holistic aspect of the Divine Feminine within us.

All this seems like a lot of work. We may, like Eeyore in *Winnie the Pooh*, think, *Why even bother to get angry? Nothing ever changes.* This is the Eeyore school of anger management. Eeyore always complains but has no hope of improvement in his life. He is fatalistic, cynical, and a bit depressed by it all. We may think there is no point in expressing anger, but we are wrong. The value in expressing anger is in releasing it from our bodies and minds. Anger unexpressed does not just disappear. It settles into the body and causes stress to the system. The more anger is suppressed, the more stress builds up.

Anger can also become our enemy when we stay stuck in it or use it as an excuse to rage at others. When anger is chosen as a habitual coping mechanism it often turns to blame, abusiveness toward ourselves or others, or staying stuck in the victim/victimizer mentality. It becomes a corpse we carry around, expending today's energy and creativity in an effort to hold on to yesterday's experience. The past becomes the present. With this strategy, we are bound in the present to the hurts of the past, and they limit our life now.

Ernest Holmes once said, "Refuse to carry the corpse of a mistaken yesterday." There is only one healing course of action to move toward in dealing with anger, and it is a rigorously challenging one. It is the course of compassion and forgiveness. Forgiveness may seem like a big concept to apply to little frustrations and hurts; we may think forgiveness is meant to be applied only to the big hurts in life. But actually, forgiveness can be applied to any upset, and the benefits are substantial. Truly letting go of an upset we feel can bring increased peace into our body and mind. It allows resolution to take place more quickly between people in a dispute. Holding on to an angry position rarely accomplishes that.

If you're *really* angry, it's likely that you can't begin to imagine feeling compassion or forgiveness for the person who did *that*. But that is exactly what you must do if you wish to be free. The overwhelming urge to express anger verbally and physically does not go away when we punish one who "deserves" it. Often the feeling that follows punishing another person is emptiness, not peace, and the real potential of expressing anger is cleansing and releasing angry feelings from the system altogether, leaving the mind and heart clear to take appropriate action to bring resolution in response to the offense.

We roar with anger, drawing attention to the offense. When we have roared sufficiently and have used up that angry energy, the natural next step is to move toward resolution of the problem. It is rare, however, that we handle our anger so cleanly and easily. When we stew over our angry feelings, refusing to express them directly, and when we rage, using our angry feelings abusively toward others, in both cases we are stuck, and being stuck perpetuates pain; it doesn't resolve it. When we are stuck in anger, we are stuck in life. We can have our grievance or we can have peace of mind, but we can't have both. Until we find our way to forgiveness, we are imprisoned in the past.

Forgiveness isn't an event—it usually doesn't happen in a moment simply because we decide to do it. Forgiveness is a process that takes time. Expressing anger doesn't mean we are unforgiving. On the contrary, feeling and expressing our anger is the crucial first step in the forgiveness process.

Most people misunderstand forgiveness and its real purpose. Forgiveness isn't given because the offending person is finally sorry, has earned it, has been sufficiently punished, or for any other reason having to do with him or her. Forgiveness is done because *you* deserve it. You deserve to be unburdened from the constant pain of carrying the past with you. To forgive another doesn't mean you condone what he did, that it was really okay, and you'll let him do it again. It is not volunteering for the doormat-of-the-month club.

Forgiveness is about setting ourselves free, and motivating us toward forgiveness is the goal of the Divine Feminine within. The Divine Feminine always pushes, nudges, and nags us to move toward balance. As long as we hold on to an old hurt, we are off-balance. We continue to be off-balance until we take some action to move our attention from focus on the hurt (past) to focus on our current goals (present). One action that shifts that focus and begins to restore balance is forgiveness. The process of getting to forgiveness may be difficult or painful. Forgiveness may stretch us into uncomfortable and unfamiliar territory that seems to move against our very nature, but in this way we learn to become more than we thought we were. In the Hindu metaphor of the goddess Kali, we might say that the fierce Kali aspect within us stirs up an angry reaction, setting a potential forgiveness process in motion that will ultimately increase our freedom and energy. The Kali cleansing anger reveals a boundary that's been violated and releases a whole history of feelings in us. Acknowledging and expressing the anger clears out past misunderstandings that have been held on to, creating a kind of soul buildup. This process can be difficult, scary, and sometimes messy. It is the chopping of Kali, an aspect of the Divine Feminine that always calls forth the fullest, highest Self within us, working to destroy our pain and resentment and reveal inner peace. When we've released anger, we are free to establish our boundaries in a more healthy way and begin again. We determine if existing boundaries still serve a good purpose. Having mended our fences, we can get on with our lives.

This is, of course, easier to think about than to do. Most often we do it in part, or not as cleanly as we might. It can take some time to make it all the way to forgiveness. Let me share a couple of examples with you to illustrate what I mean.

Andrea, an acquaintance who had married for the second time, was talking with me over lunch about her intense feelings of anger at her former spouse. After their divorce, during a period of shared child custody, her former spouse was experiencing mental instability, unbeknownst to Andrea. The problem became apparent when their toddler returned to Andrea's home after a visit with his father, and called out in his sleep, "Don't hurt me, Daddy! Please don't hurt me! I promise I'll be good!"

This broke Andrea's heart, and feelings of rage arose within her toward her son's father. The custody situation was addressed and changed, and my friend became her son's primary custodial parent. In time the father's mental health improved, and the child seemed to have recovered from his trauma. But Andrea clearly had not. Her lingering rage affected her relationship with her second husband and his children and former wife, as she projected her rage and her negative assumptions about previous spouses onto her new husband's family situation, too.

This rage was important to Andrea, because to her it was evidence that she loved her son tremendously. She felt that her former husband had been very wrong in his behavior toward their child, and that she was more than justified in her feelings and behavior. But while he had, indeed, been wrong, Andrea's attachment to keeping her anger alive was taking a toll on her current relationships. This kind of rage was a familiar pattern in her life, and so Andrea never fully addressed it, never released it, and never found ways to deal with new anger appropriately when it came up. Andrea pushed the voice of the Divine Feminine to the back of her awareness, where her inner imbalance continued to cry out to be addressed and corrected. Her second marriage also ended in divorce.

But that isn't the end of the process for Andrea. The inner voice of the Divine Feminine will rise again and again in her until she faces it honestly and recognizes that the way in which she habitually handles anger is not only ineffective but also damaging. Andrea's rage damages not only the one at whom it is directed but the children she loves and her own body as well. If she chooses to face this, she will be in the frightening realm of the unknown. She will have no idea what to do. In surrendering to the unknown, Andrea could become truly open to learning. In the learning, she could become more whole.

A second story ends much differently. Richard, a longtime member of the church, came into my office one afternoon to share a profound experience he had had. I knew Richard had been seriously injured in a car accident the year before, but I had never heard the full story. I learned that afternoon that what had happened to Richard was no accident.

One beautiful evening, Richard was taking his wife to a dance program at a theater in our area. They were elegantly dressed and looking forward to a fabulous evening. Deep in conversation, Richard missed his turn and had to drive quite a distance before he could find a place to turn around. The place he found was a parking lot with a long two-lane entrance corridor into it. In a hurry, he rushed down the corridor, turned, and was heading out, when suddenly he was assailed by loud honking, yelling, and bright headlights in his rearview mirror. A car full of angry young men was right on his rear bumper. As he looked into his rearview mirror, they looked crazed. He sped up, but they stayed right with him, intentionally bumping his car. He moved left into the other lane to get out of their way. When they swerved to try and hit his car, he moved even farther to the left, so far, in fact, that tire marks remained later on the far left curb where he had hit it.

The other car finally sped past him, and Richard thought, *Well, they got what they wanted—got their laughs. They ran me off the road.* He stopped and got out of his car to see if there was any damage to his vehicle, but the attack wasn't over. The car full of young men stopped at the end of the corridor, parking sideways across Richard's lane, blocking his exit. They began to get out of their car.

Richard is a big, strong middle-aged man, not someone the average fellow would try to take on alone. "Rev. Mary, where I grew up people fought with their fists. No one carried guns. And the idea was, if more than one guy was coming for you and you were big, you'd run at them to attack first. If you were lucky they'd be surprised and run. If not, you hoped you could knock the first guy down before the others got there and they'd back off. So that's what I did. Without really thinking about it, I ran at the car! And the two guys who'd been getting out of the back doors got back in and the car sped away. *Great! It worked!* I thought, and I headed back to my car. Now all my attention was on my wife. Was she okay? That's the last thing I remember. I didn't even see or hear their car coming."

Richard's wife, Pamela, says the attack car hit him going about thirty miles per hour. Richard hit the windshield and flew up over the car, landing fifty feet away on the pavement behind it. The car sped away once again, leaving him lying in a pool of blood, with blood trickling out of his nose. Pamela knew his injuries were serious and, as she prayed, she kept saying to Richard, "Don't leave me! Don't leave me!"

The police officer who was first on the scene told Richard later, "I've seen a lot of these things. When I saw you in that pool of blood I thought to myself, *This one's not gonna make it.*" But Richard did make it. He is fortunate to be so big and muscular, because, as he described it, "I was picking glass out of my neck for a long time."

Richard had a lot of healing to do, not only in body but in mind and heart. He was enraged, and his anger was so profound that he told a friend that he was going to buy a gun to protect himself and his family. "This will never happen to me again," Richard stated, "it'll be *blam, blam,* and ask questions later." His friend Joe listened to Richard's fury. "Joe was so wise," Richard said with a smile. "He took me to the store to buy the gun, and he made me tell the guy there that the reason I wanted it was to kill human beings if I was attacked. We were there about half an hour when I said, 'Maybe I'm not ready to do this yet. Let's think about it a little longer,' and we left to get some lunch."

At the restaurant, Carrie, a waitress and friend of both Richard's and Joe's, told them how her son and his girlfriend had been attacked recently by a man who was drunk. Carrie's son had been seriously hurt in the encounter. "I got really angry again," Richard said, "and Joe looked at me wisely over his coffee, and said, 'So, Richard, should we go back and buy that gun now?' That was when I knew having a gun was the wrong choice for me."

After the police caught and arrested the driver of the car

that ran Richard down, Richard had to decide whether to go to the sentencing hearing. He finally decided that he would, and told me, "Rev. Mary, you know how Spirit works. I went up the elevator in the courthouse alone, and the doors opened on a completely empty corridor right in front of the courtroom where the sentencing was going to happen. Completely empty, except for one person sitting all alone in the hall. The defendant. Just me and him in an empty hallway. And I thought, *Okay, God, what do you want me to do here?* Mary, there was *no one* anywhere around us. I mean, I could've killed him if I'd wanted to. And all the time I was asking God for guidance as I walked over to him.

"I sat down beside him and asked if we were supposed to wait in the hall. 'Well,' he said, 'the judge and the public defender aren't here yet, so we have to wait for them.' They kept us waiting for *four hours!* In that time," Richard went on, "he and I began to talk. I asked him if he'd ever thought how in the few minutes that our lives had overlapped everything had changed for both of us. 'I think about it all the time,' he said, 'I was so stupid! I thought the best thing to do was get tanked up with my friends and drive around raising hell. I'm not religious, and I won't pretend that I am, but while I was in jail waiting for the hearing I had a lot of time to think and to read the Bible. One of the things I read in there said that if you lie to a man, you can restore him by telling him the truth. And if you steal from him, you can restore him by giving back what you took. But if you take his life, there's no way you can restore him. I just keep thinking that I almost took your life. I know this probably doesn't mean much, but for whatever it's worth, I'm sorry for the pain I've caused you and your family.' "

Richard said, "Now, Rev. Mary, that was the last thing I expected to hear from this guy. We kept talking, and I told him, 'I have to believe there's a purpose to all this, because you and I have sure gone through a lot of trouble for each other to learn whatever lessons we need to learn from this.' His eyebrows kind of went up at that," Richard laughed. "He wasn't expecting to hear anything like that from me, either. I asked him if he wanted some coffee, and we agreed to go to the coffee shop together. His girlfriend was there by that time, and she and a couple friends of his went with us. We talked about our lives and the night of the attack. We even joked about how odd it was that we were talking like this, and that when it was all over we could probably make a lot of money going on Oprah together. Then he got quiet. He told me he was afraid of going to the penitentiary. He'd heard that most guys who've been there once end up going back again. When it was time for the sentencing, we all got up to go back upstairs. His girlfriend was crying.

"At the courtroom door, the defendant held the door open for his family and everyone going into the courtroom," Richard told me, "and I waited till they'd all gone in before I came to the door. 'Listen,' I said to him, 'you told me you're afraid to go to the penitentiary. I don't see that for you. I see a lot of good in you, and I just want you to hear it from me, that I believe in you.' The young guy's eyes filled with tears, and he said, 'I never thought I'd be able to ask you this, but would you shake my hand?' I did," Richard said, "and then embraced him. We both went in to the courtroom, and I went up to sit with my attorney. I told her what had happened, and that I wasn't sure now that I would stay for the sentencing. 'You might want to stay,' she told me. 'The judge hasn't made up his mind about the sentence in this case, yet. You could say something to him.' 'No,' I told her, 'I don't have anything to say,' and I stood up to go.

" 'Mr. Esterbrook,' the judge said to me, 'are you leaving?' 'Yes, Your Honor, I am,' I answered. 'I'd like to ask you a few questions before you go,' he said. And he asked me to tell him about my medical bills and condition and how this had affected my family. And I answered his questions and told him about the problems, and that I was in pain all the time. 'What kind of retribution would you like to see in this case?' he asked me. He actually used that word, 'retribution'! I told him, 'Your Honor, that's why I'm glad this is your job. I don't want to have anything to do with any kind of retribution. That's your decision, not mine.' The judge looked kind of surprised and said, 'Thank you, Mr. Esterbrook, you can go.' And as I left, instead of walking around my attorney's table and out the gate, I walked the long way behind the defendant's table and just touched him on the back as I went past him and down toward the door past his family.

"My attorney called me later and she said that she'd had the opportunity to tell the judge that the defendant and I had had time to talk, and had come to a kind of peace with each other culminating in an embrace. She told me, though, that the judge had let the guy off too easy, sending him back to jail instead of the penitentiary. But in my heart I knew that it was just right.

"Now, my brother doesn't agree with me at all on this, but I feel real peace about it. Forgiveness is so powerful! It's so powerful. It's not the thing we're all after. The thing we're after is love. But forgiveness is the bridge. It's the bridge that gets us there. Sometimes when I wake up in the morning now and Pam is still asleep with the light just falling on her face, I reach out and gently touch her hair. Because I'm *here*—because I can."

When Richard finished, both of us were in tears. The atmosphere in my office had taken on a hushed holiness, as if it were filled with angels. Richard apologized for taking so much of my time in telling the story. "Are you kidding?" I replied. "This experience has blessed my day. I'm so glad you came in to talk with me."

I hope you feel similarly blessed by reading Richard's story. Cynics may point to the driver of the car and say that everyone gets religion when faced with jail time. The point of the story, though, is not about the transformation of the defendant, but the transformation that Richard experienced from bondage and pain to freedom and peace.

Forgiveness is indeed a powerful thing. It is not our first impulse to forgive. It requires intention and willingness to reach out, when the opportunity arises, past the hurt and anger to create a bridge made of genuine listening from compassion.

There is no predicting what will occur if we make the uncomfortable choice of reaching out to one who has hurt us. We feel vulnerable, as Richard did, when we consider offering kindness to someone who has caused us pain. But what we're actually doing is making ourselves available to the Guidance of the Divine Feminine, that deeper wisdom within us that knows what to do, even when it seems out of sync with our defense systems. When we open the door to the Divine Feminine, miracles can happen, because we have invited them in. Kali has awakened in us the awareness that a boundary has been violated. She has flashed through us as anger to be appropriately expressed and released. She has revealed information about our best and worst selves in the process and given us the opportunity to choose which self will take the lead once the anger has been felt and expressed. If we follow the lead of the Divine Feminine, we find we can choose our best self and let ourselves have the freedom, peace, and love that follow.

Not all of us are as intractable as Andrea or as open as Richard, but these examples serve to clearly show the results of the choices we make in our own lives regarding anger and compassion. Our situations and the results of our actions may be more subtle than these, but the bottom line is the same. Holding on to old resentments and hurts binds our lives and causes us continuing problems. Practicing forgiveness sets us free.

Anger opens the gateway to the bridge of forgiveness. Anger alerts us to the recognition that forgiveness is called for. Feeling that anger is an essential part of the healing process. It isn't a stage we can skip. We can pretend we've forgiven without ever acknowledging the anger we feel. But true forgiveness first acknowledges *all* of the depth of the hurt that was felt and then moves to releasing it with compassion for ourselves and the other. We can't release what we pretend isn't there. We must consciously choose constructive action to do the releasing.

Once we've been set free in true forgiveness, it doesn't matter who agrees or disagrees with our choice to forgive. The experience of bondage or freedom isn't theirs but ours, and we feel its precious value. The Divine Feminine within us knows this, and knows we deserve to be free. Every experience of anger and frustration is an opportunity to enter this freedom.

I believe that forgiveness arises as a viable choice when we have sufficiently grieved over an offense. Some people are able to quickly choose to let the offense go, but for many of us, it takes some time. There are steps that can help us get there. The first step is to deal with feelings that arise *at the time of the offense*—usually these are sadness or anger. We will experience both, if we let ourselves; sometimes one at a time, sometimes both together. A good listener is helpful, as is some action that expresses your feelings. The action can be shedding tears, chopping wood, exercise, writing unedited letters (never to be mailed!), slamming doors, or any action that doesn't hurt you or anyone else yet is a satisfying way of getting your feelings to move from the inside to the outside.

There is a pressure release that occurs from giving anger an avenue of expression, but in order for this to be fully effective we must also be willing to *let the anger go*. For some of us who are really attached to our angry feelings, we may rant and rave over them without a sense of relief or release until we can take some action that directly connects with the offending person. We may need to talk with that person right away about what occurred. If you are someone for whom expressing your feelings with a neutral person isn't enough to trigger that feeling of release, be aware that dumping on the offending person may not bring about a satisfactory ending to the situation that's bothering you. First try out what you want to say with a neutral friend and accept some feedback about how your communication comes across. Could it lead to resolution, or is it inflammatory? When you have a bit of perspective on what you intend to say, go ahead and do it. Then you and the offender can move on to the next step.

Whether you express your anger through a process, to a neutral friend, or directly to the person involved in the upset, once the pressure of holding the anger inside is released, you may be able to more clearly evaluate what needs to happen next. Recognizing and expressing the feeling of anger doesn't prevent a recurrence. The second step on the forgiveness path is to examine the boundary that has been crossed through the offense. Is that boundary realistic? Is it serving you in a healthy way? Does it accurately reflect your needs? And, most important, are you communicating it fairly to others? There is a lot more peace between us and others when we can clearly ask for what we want and hear a no as well as a yes. If we feel free to ask, and give others the freedom to respond honestly, we can also extend to others the freedom to ask, and extend to ourselves the freedom to respond honestly with a yes or no. Alan Cohen, author of *Rising in Love,* wisely points out that a kind no is a more loving response to another's request than a resentful yes. When we allow ourselves and others to honestly communicate our needs, and to honestly respond about what we are able and willing to do, we know where we stand in relationship. We are responsibly tending our own boundaries, not codependently expecting someone else to tend them for us by reading our minds and requesting of us only that which we want to do. Part of our work as adults is to learn to handle clear communication with others.

There is a third step, too. Once we've experienced our emotions and examined our boundaries, we must assess the state of the relationship where the boundary was violated. The relationship breach is not healed by actions taken to let out the feelings. It is still in a broken state due to the offense. We must decide whether or not the relationship is still viable. Sometimes it isn't. Can this person learn to respect you and your boundaries? Can you continue to communicate clearly when something unacceptable occurs? Can you allow this person to do the same with you? Can you trust each other to treat the other's feelings and needs with respect? If so, you need to mutually outline how you'll handle situations like this one in the future.

Letting go of the need to punish another, no longer feeling an emotional pull at the memory of the hurtful event, and wishing the best for the other means we have finally come to a place of relative peace and forgiveness. This is not the same as reestablishing the relationship with the same closeness and privilege as before. You may feel this isn't a friendship you wish to continue. You may choose to continue the acquaintance in a more casual way than before. You can forgive the person and still make choices like these.

Franco, a man in our church, had lost a young daughter in a hit-and-run drunk-driving accident. Franco was angered by one of my sermons on forgiveness, feeling it would be disloyal to the memory of Jill, his beloved daughter, to forgive the woman who drove the car that killed her. It was difficult for Franco to understand that it was all right for him to have a full life following the death of his child, and that doing so didn't mean he loved her less or remembered her with less devotion. And he didn't need to befriend the driver of the car in order to forgive her. Rather, Franco needed to release the dreams he'd had for Jill's life. Releasing them would require feeling all of his sadness and anger, letting those emotions out, and moving on.

Forgiveness requires releasing—releasing pain from the past that persists in the present, releasing the need to place blame and to punish. Letting go results in freeing ourselves to get on with our lives, trusting that each one of us is in our right place, even when we can't understand how that could be true in our present circumstances.

We are part of the divine organization of universal harmony at each moment, even in those moments that look less than perfect. Usually we cannot grasp the vast whole and our place in it with any degree of clarity. Thomas Troward, an English judge who wrote and lectured at the turn of the century, once wrote that as God is omnipresent, God's presence is the only true reality. Harmony, Troward believed, had to be an essential component of God, or else God would be self-destructive. To me, this means that even when my personal world seems completely out of harmony, this disharmony fits with the whole somehow, in ways larger than my understanding, and will eventually return to a balance even I can recognize, if I learn to cooperate with the wisdom within me rather than become lost in despair. There are times when I must bring my best to the moment and trust Spirit to do the rest.

We must stop when a momentous event occurs, and honestly recognize that it has affected us. We must pay attention to our bodies for the clues they give us. The Divine Feminine is grounded in the rhythms of the earth, and this includes our bodies. The Divine Feminine often uses physical symptoms to get our attention when we have shut down the emotional responses that usually would tell us how we feel. Do you have headaches? insomnia? stomach or back aches? Is your appetite off? Does your heart pound or your palms sweat? Are you irritable? If you experience such symptoms without an accompanying emotion, they may be indicators that your body is experiencing a feeling your mind has been refusing to recognize. If so, it may be time to consider what those underlying emotions could be. It may be time to enter into grief or anger willingly and give these feelings voice so you can move on. It may be time to forgive, setting yourself free in the process.

Now let's turn to the third type of anger-provoking situation I described at the beginning of the chapter, one in which anger arises from the violation of or disrespect toward some cherished value. Our values are formed over a period of time through the influence of our families, friends, teachers, and life experiences. It isn't only what these people say and do that shapes our values but the ways in which we interpret and judge their behavior and its outcomes. It isn't only the individual things that happen in our lives that influence the conclusions we come to about life but how they fit in to all the life experience we have up to that point, and the decisions we've already made about life and other people. Our values are an extremely complex interwoven matrix that is inextricably linked to our friends, our work, and our sense of self.

For this reason, threats or perceived threats to these values generate visceral defense responses in most of us. To discover ourselves to be wrong in our fundamental, long-held beliefs would cost more than simply the embarrassment of changing our minds. Many times the repercussions of changing our minds would change everything else in our lives as well. The cost of actual change can be great, and even when we aren't consciously aware of all that is threatened by a person challenging our values by their behavior, our emotional reaction can be significant. The rage we can feel at someone we don't even know whose point of view is very different from our own is tragically played out in church burnings, hate crimes against racial and sexual minorities, the murder of doctors who perform abortions, and politically motivated violence like the bombing of the federal building in Oklahoma City.

Underneath our rage is fear. Our familiar, comfortable life—or life the way we envision it can become—is threatened by the behavior of a person or group. We fear if others are allowed to continue to speak or act as they have been, something precious could be lost or destroyed. Fear motivates our fight-or-flight response, and many times we may come out swinging—verbally with our cronies, if not physically against the perceived enemy.

A film was made in northern California a number of years ago called *The Color of Fear*. This film, shown at a meeting of church leadership, had a profound effect on me. When it was over, I found that I couldn't stop weeping. In it, a group of men meet together over a number of days to discuss racism.

They are black, Latino, Asian, and white. Initially all of the men present understand that racism toward nonwhite people is still a difficult problem, with the exception of one of the white men. Although the men of color explain to him, first patiently and then with increasing emotion, their own personal, abundant experiences with racism, this man continues to believe that among his own circle of friends such racism is nonexistent. A number of times he makes obviously racist statements himself but is oblivious to it—exactly the point the other members of the group are trying to get across. Many white folks don't realize their own racism because they are so unaware of the cultures and lives of nonwhite people. As the days of discussion go on, this man begins to understand, and he commits to living his life differently. We find out later in the film that doing so has changed his life, including costing him some friendships. Letting go of cherished beliefs and values does not come cheap, and this is why we defend them with such vehemence and why so much violence is perpetrated over them.

I wept after the film because I realized that some assumptions I had made about the life of a friend of mine from Panama, who was also a member of this leadership group, were not based on knowledge of her life at all. I felt I had not truly honored our friendship, that by my assumptions I had prevented myself from really knowing her. We spent some time together after the film talking about those assumptions and about the need I had discovered to become aware of my own ignorance in order to truly hear and understand people of races different from my own.

In spite of the power of that experience, it is still difficult for me to feel open to hearing the point of view of people with whom I strongly disagree. And this seems to be what many of us feel when someone opposes our "important" opinions. We need a way to stand aside and get some breathing room from our own point of view in order to cultivate more peace and less anger—in ourselves and in our world. As a bumper sticker challenges us, "Don't believe everything you think."

In Stephen Covey's book *First Things First* he describes a classroom of MBA students polarized over the issue of abortion. Covey had each side choose a representative to argue the issue, and he provided the two verbal combatants with some challenging guidelines: commit to communicating until they come up with a win-win solution, don't give in, don't compromise, don't capitulate, and seek first to understand—no responding with counterarguments until the listener can restate the speaker's point in such a way that the speaker feels understood. Covey then coached the students in their discussion to help them keep the guidelines in place. The entire class witnessed a breakthrough when the two debaters finally began to really listen to each other, suddenly understanding the *feelings* (not just the ideas) behind the other's strong opinion and value. Upon discovering what it meant to really listen, people on both sides felt ashamed of having labeled, judged, and condemned those who thought differently than themselves. Some even commented, "Now we understand why they feel the way they do."

What happened here? On a very basic level, the combatants became less afraid of each other as their knowledge grew, and therefore less angry. Each came to understand why the other's point of view was so important to him, and how he came to feel and think the way he did. At a fundamental level, the students forgave each other for holding different opinions because they understood much more of what went into that opinion than when they began. A meaningful basis for genuine, respectful listening and dialogue was established. From that place, a synthesis of opinions could occur, and a new solution not apparent at the beginning of a discussion could be revealed. Anger rooted in conflicting values can begin to be resolved through deep, patient listening. We may discover information previously unknown to us that could change our own position or provide missing information for our opponent, once we understand his thinking and feelings in relation to his experience and facts, and we know he understands ours.

Disagreements are exacerbated when the participants refuse to fully listen to each other. The rigidity and disrespect shown by interrupting and talking over another person accomplishes very little in the way of creating understanding. Most television talk shows are not models for genuine conflict resolution. While listening for understanding is hard work and requires patience and flexibility in the midst of significant emotional reactions, it holds rich promise for progress at impasses arising from a conflict of values.

At the very least, anger and violence can be reduced through understanding the experience and thinking of another person who seems so very different from ourselves. When we understand that person's life better, our sense of being personally offended and threatened by him diminishes. We "forgive" his offense when we see life for a moment through his eyes, because we realize there is nothing to forgive. No offense has been committed. His opinion is not about us personally, it relates to him and his own life. When we see his life experience with respect, though we may not agree with his conclusions, we do away with the need for violence because we begin to create space for another to be heard. Out of that deep, authentic listening and speaking, new solutions are born.

Einstein is credited with having said, "We can't solve problems by using the same kind of thinking we used when we created them." When we see beyond our familiar beliefs and values into those of others, we discover that our willingness to hear needn't be experienced as a threat but can create useful, synergistic solutions to the profound challenges we face today. We must forgive others for seeing the world differently than we do to get to real resolution. We must hear them out and finally understand what's behind their stated opinions. We must be heard ourselves, and share what's behind our stated opinions. When we do these things in our personal life, we create an opening for others to learn how to do this in their lives. The growth of such a practice can transform our world, spilling over into the workplace and into our civic and governmental interactions as well.

Once again, we find the Divine Feminine at the root of this deep listening. Such behavior is an affirmation of our essential connectedness, a oneness that is the ground of being for all of us. Wholeness, oneness, harmony at the root of all life — no matter what the appearance of the moment — these are the teachings of the Divine Feminine. Despite the appearance of abundant differences in people, mystical religious traditions from all over the world affirm that all things and all people are intimately connected.

To summarize, then, anger holds a promise of the possibility of healing through forgiveness and understanding. These qualities can bring a powerful and fresh approach to resolving the most serious breakdowns between people and nations in our world today. Although responding in this way is not our first impulse when anger is triggered, by listening to the inner Guidance of the Divine Feminine in those angry moments, we can find enormous potential for synergistic solutions to these breakdowns when we choose to practice deep listening, forgiveness, and understanding.

Four

From Brokenness to the Discovery of Wholeness

....

For several centuries, down through many dynasties, a village was known for its exquisite and fragile porcelain. Especially striking were its urns: high as tables, wide as chairs, they were admired around the globe for their strong form and delicate beauty.

Legend has it that when each urn was finished, there was one final step. The artist broke it and then put it back together with gold filigree. An ordinary urn was then transformed into a priceless work of art. What seemed finished wasn't . . . until it was broken.

> —*Robert Kriegel and Louis Patler,*
> If It Ain't Broke . . . Break It!

Getting divorced, releasing a child for adoption, being fired, flunking a class, experiencing infertility or bankruptcy or serious injury or illness: each of these, in its own way, can cause the person experiencing it to feel broken. Brokenness is the shocking experience of discovering that a goal you had pinned your hopes on, or a condition you counted on as an ongoing part of your life, is suddenly, irrevocably gone. Loss is the generic word we use to describe the brokenness of having no choice but to surrender something we want to hold on to. Losses show up in our lives in large and small ways all the time. We may feel the loss of a lifelong dream that we realize will never come true, or be forced to say good-bye to an actual person or thing.

Regardless of the form, once a loss is acknowledged as real and permanent, our lives change. The spiritual practice of surrendering in the face of brokenness is one of the most powerful ways to learn to trust the Divine Feminine in our lives.

Breaking is painful not only because of losing something precious to us but also because our larger life itself feels broken. Our sense of who we are and our relationship to life itself are shattered. We no longer know what to expect or trust. It is most disorienting.

Friends and family often want to help, yet we may find it hard to receive their support, because we are so numbed by the shock of what's happened. In some cases, our loved ones may not even realize that the loss we've experienced is a significant blow. Observed from outside, the full impact of the loss may not be obvious to others. This can leave us feeling more lonely than ever, but with little energy or will to ask for help or correct people's impressions with explanations. Additionally there is sometimes the feeling of embarrassment, shame, or failure associated with loss. In our goal-oriented culture, "losers" are not often portrayed as people to emulate or to feel sympathy for, and when we feel like losers, as we often do when part of our life has suddenly fallen apart, we may go into hiding to prevent others from knowing too much. We avoid their possible judgment and pity, perhaps feeling that either of these would only add insult to injury, or perhaps because we can't bear the idea that we have let down our loved ones.

But, like each area of challenge we have examined thus far, there are possibilities that appear with the shattering of some aspect of our life. When recognized, taking hold of these possibilities can provide the "gold filigree" that glues us back together—perhaps even more beautifully than before the loss.

In indigenous cultures that practice shamanism, dramatic shattering experiences in a person's life can be looked upon as an initiation. Such experiences may come about spontaneously or may be intentionally brought about by the initiation ceremonies of the tribe. The intention and common result for the initiate, in cultures equipped to interpret these shattering experiences as power-giving rites, is a kind of ego death. That is, the initiate can no longer view herself in the way she did before the experience. She is changed by the shattering into an expanded version of herself. Within the tribe, a person surviving such an ego-death experience is seen to have been reborn and may then be considered to be a novice shaman with mysterious powers, worthy of increased respect and increased responsibility for the welfare of the community.

In Western culture, we do not have this kind of empowering vision through which to interpret the meaning of profound losses. Nevertheless we can choose to look at these experiences as opportunities, once again, for us to understand things from a different point of view. If our shattering itself can be seen as a possible opening to a larger life and a more empowered self, we may find that the other side of loss reveals a new awareness of the gifts in our lives, and the ability to more deeply appreciate them. It may develop in us an increased ability to trust that new experiences are coming to replace the loss in our life, and that they will be valuable and good, even if very different from the life we lived and loved before the loss. As André Gide writes, "It is one of life's laws that as soon as one door closes, another opens. But the tragedy is that we look at the closed door and disregard the open one."

Sadly, we don't even notice the open door when we insist on fixing our gaze upon the closed door, pounding on it and begging it to open once again. Rev. Terry Cole Whittaker told a story some years ago that illuminates the idea that when we lose what we value, it is best to open up to that which can sustain us now, rather than remaining focused in the past. In Rev. Terry's story, a rat is put into a maze in which there is a piece of cheese at the end of one of the pathways. By using its nose, in a sequence of trial and error, the rat eventually finds the cheese. The second time in the maze, if the cheese is in the same place, the rat finds it much more quickly, and by the third time, the rat goes directly to it. In later trials, if the cheese is removed from the familiar place, the rat goes to where the cheese has been for two or three subsequent attempts, then finally, when placed in the maze, the rat begins searching for food systematically from the beginning of the maze until it finds the cheese in its new place. Human beings are the only species, Rev. Terry says, who continue to go to the old familiar place long after the "cheese" has been removed. Instead of beginning the search again, she says, we return to the old place again and again, shake our fist at the sky, and exclaim, "Where the hell's the cheese?!" We may miss the "cheese" that is available in a new place by remaining focused on what was once there but no longer can be found in the old place or in the old way.

Times of brokenness are shocking and difficult. In the midst of them we are likely to experience an emotional roller coaster. From hope to despair; from bargaining to blaming; from rage to guilt; from terror to peace—loss rockets us from one emotion to the next with little rest or comfort. Just when we think we have regained our balance, the rug seems to be pulled out from under us and the cycle of emotions begins again.

This can be what it feels like when a circumstance crumbles us slowly, rather than shattering us all at once, as it did in Andy's life. Andy, a regular at my Wednesday night prayer and meditation service, was struggling. The business he owned had made piles of money in the 1980s but was going under in the early 1990s. A man of high integrity, Andy wanted more than anything to keep all his employees busy and paid, to pay all his creditors, to be kind and generous to his debtors, and to fulfill work he had promised on budget and on time. Yet everything seemed to be conspiring against him. Daily the pressures mounted. Andy was forced to let go of contracts and employees, to negotiate over and over again with his creditors as work got slower and slower. On top of this he was in the midst of a bitter divorce, and his wife felt that all of his troubles were manufactured to prevent her from receiving her financial due in the settlement.

At our evening service Andy requested prayer on a weekly basis for Divine Guidance for the right actions to take and the courage to trust in and follow the Guidance he received. As Albert Schweitzer once wrote, "The hardest thing I've ever had to do is to follow the guidance I prayed for." After months of struggle, when Andy had tried everything he could think of, he surrendered. Andy turned his business over to the Infinite. He stopped trying to control and figure out the answers himself; instead he listened to the inner voice of the Divine Feminine that he had been resisting so painfully for so long. Andy knew within days that he had to shut down his business and declare bankruptcy. This felt to him like the greatest failure of his life. He was crushed, broken, and he felt that Spirit had abandoned him.

But Andy was amazed to find that once he surrendered and acknowledged what needed to be done, Life rushed in to support him. After closing the business he helped find placements for his former employees. Having no idea how he would make ends meet, Andy began to trust each day to Spirit. His thoughts and mood began to lift. Work was offered to him. His divorce was finalized. Andy's faith in the goodness of people began to be restored. The Divine Feminine drew together the new threads of his life, but it couldn't have done that had Andy refused to surrender.

Today Andy is relaxed and happy. He is pleasantly surprised each day at how far he has come because he chose to surrender rather than carrying an unbearable weight all alone. Now Andy generously participates in church activities and offers others the encouragement he has received. Being attached to the belief that he had to do it all himself had caused Andy no end of pain, but allowing the Divine Feminine to guide him toward a new way of living brought him peace of mind and happiness.

I have marveled in the past at hearing prestigious speakers claim that their most devastating experiences of being shattered have become their greatest blessings. Today I strongly suspect that this potential for blessing exists in all our experiences of shattering. *The only difference between seizing the blessing and overlooking it entirely may be the way in which we look at the experience.*

If you were mediocre at sports, as many kids are, you remember what it felt like to be chosen last for a team or to be the least-skilled player. When my son, Luke, was a junior in high school, he had his first opportunity to run varsity for the cross-country team at his high school in one of the most important final invitational meets of the year. Luke was loyal, dependable, and persistent, and though not among the fastest runners, he really wanted to make a good showing at this race. My son is very tall and strong, yet he quickly fell back in his race. One by one the other runners crossed the finish line. No Luke. When he finally entered the stadium, Luke was alone. Every other runner had already finished, yet he pushed on, holding his own pace.

High school males display big egos in their conversations and behavior, but in truth their egos are quite fragile. Losing is tough, and coming in last is the hardest of all. As my son approached me after the meet, I wondered how he'd feel about the race and about his performance. Luke smiled gamely and greeted me with a proud, "I PRed (beat his own personal record) by one second, Mom!" His spirit and courage really touched my heart. In spite of the difficulty of being last, Luke chose to identify what was positive about what he had accomplished. He chose to acknowledge and honor his own effort. Luke heard the Divine Feminine whispering encouragement to keep going in the face of certain defeat. He could have chosen not to finish the race at all—to simply stop running, walk the rest of the way, and avoid that painful lone entrance into the stadium. But the voice within told him not to quit—he could finish the race and uphold the commitment of his whole team to the meet. Luke's experience as a runner has added to his empathy for those who persist in the face of difficult odds, as well as those who become the negative focus of attention because of their handicaps or differences. Continuing in spite of being last taught him that he has the resilience to finish, and to benefit from the experience.

We are quick to label experiences that humble or break us as bad and wrong, but what if our assessment of them is incomplete? Few people would actively choose to experience the pain of loss, yet those very experiences may provide us with transformational openings that can improve our lives forever. Our interpretation of who we are and what such shattering experiences mean can affect us for the rest of our lives. No one controls how we think about these things except ourselves, and we can choose to think encouragingly and gently rather than harshly. If we do, we can recover from loss more easily.

An old tale illustrates the power of our interpretation of events. A farmer with a single horse wakes up one morning to find his horse has broken through the fence in the pasture and is gone. "What terrible luck!" his neighbors all exclaim. "Maybe," says the farmer, "maybe not." The next day his horse returns, bringing a herd of wild horses with him. "What amazingly good luck!" say the neighbors. "Maybe. Maybe not," the farmer says again. The following day while trying to break one of the wild horses, the farmer's only son is thrown and breaks his leg. Once again the neighbors all cry, "Oh, no! The worst possible luck!" But the farmer doggedly replies again, "Maybe, maybe not." War breaks out and the army marches into town the following day conscripting all the young men for service, but the farmer's son is ineligible because of his broken leg. "Tremendous luck!" the neighbors enviously comment. The farmer just smiles.

At what point was the farmer's luck actually good or bad? At what point in our lives do we stop and declare them broken? Because we never know what's coming next, it's difficult to say how a shattering experience today may contribute to an unforeseen blessing tomorrow. Awareness of that possibility may help us stay open to the unknown.

My journey into personal brokenness was one that led to an unforeseen blessing as well. The journey began on July 17, 1997. For several weeks preceding my vacation, which was to begin on July 5, a back problem had begun to nag at me. Although I was icing my back from time to time, I felt I was simply too busy with vital matters at work to take time to see my chiropractor or carve out time in my schedule to exercise. I ignored the inner prompting of the voice of the Divine Feminine as it told me I needed to stop what I was doing and take some serious time to rejuvenate. That was not the only message of my inner voice, as you will see, but it was the one I was most actively aware of ignoring at the time.

My last task before a well-earned month away was to perform a wedding on Independence Day at a beautiful home in Laguna Beach, California, on an outdoor deck overlooking the Pacific Ocean. I didn't know then that it would be my last official act as a minister for a very long time.

The vacation plan beginning on July 5 had a number of

parts. With my dear friend, Amanda, I set off driving toward Oregon from southern California. We were to meet another friend in Ashland and spend a few days at the Oregon Shakespeare Festival before heading north to a tiny town nestled into the northern Oregon coast. There we would spend the next few weeks in a small cabin taking day trips all over the area.

We enjoyed the beginning of the trip and our stop in Ashland, and made it to the coast by July 10. For a week we visited the little coastal towns, had wonderful meals, shopped, went for long walks in the woods, and rode our bikes. But the stress of the preceding months didn't let up easily. I was still tense and worried over several unfinished projects at the church, and my back was not improving.

On the morning of July 17, I was particularly uncomfortable. We were to drive in to Portland to have lunch with a good friend, Rev. Jody Miller Stevenson, and a couple of other acquaintances. We made the two-hour drive to the city with me riding in the passenger seat in a reclining position with ice under my lower back. I was in pain throughout the drive and the luncheon, and felt very distracted and preoccupied by the discomfort, not to mention worried that I seemed to be getting worse.

Jody was aware of my discomfort, and after lunch took me to see her chiropractor. He told me that I had several muscles in tight spasm and did his best to try to ease them. We stayed at Jody's home for dinner, but by that time I couldn't stand or sit without great discomfort. I ate sitting on the floor and finally had to try lying down. Nothing helped, and Amanda and I decided we'd better start back to our cabin.

For three to four hours after we got back to Manzanita, I writhed in agony, trying every position, including walking and kneeling, to ease my excruciating pain. Then at 2:00 A.M., I woke Amanda and told her I didn't think I could take it any longer. "Should we call the hospital?" she asked me. I thought for only a moment and said, "Yes." The nearest hospital was Tillamook County General, about forty minutes away. They told us to come in, and as I didn't think I could sit up in the car at all, Amanda called an ambulance.

By the time the paramedics arrived I was in too much pain for them to move me onto a stretcher and into the ambulance, so they gave me a shot of morphine and waited. It took about thirty minutes and three more doses of different medications before the pain began to let up.

As we drove to the hospital, Jon, one of the paramedics, rode in the back with me. Finally feeling free of pain, I chatted with him about his work. Being a paramedic for twenty years had been very satisfying work, Jon told me, because in almost all cases his patients felt better by the time they reached the hospital. Most people, he went on to say, would be out cold with the amount of pain medication I had received. "Unfortunately everything we gave you is going to your pain," he said. "I'm so sorry you have to be going through this." His compassion was very comforting.

At the emergency room, X-rays showed that I had very little cushioning between three of my vertebrae, but there was no conclusive, observable reason they could see for the terrible pain. I was sent home with a medication usually given to dental patients who have just had their wisdom teeth extracted. I was feeling very sleepy and dozed a little as we drove home, but by the time we reached our cabin I was beginning to feel the pain more acutely again. It was almost 5:00 A.M.

By midafternoon the next day I called the hospital and talked to a nurse since the pain was almost as bad as the night before. On her recommendation, I returned to the hospital emergency room. While trying to get into the provided wheelchair, I moved in such a way that I triggered even more terrible pain, and I involuntarily began to scream, unable to sit down or straighten up. It was a strange sensation over which I had no control. I heard myself screaming, knowing it was my body's only way to release the terrible pain. I observed it, but I couldn't stop. I thought of all the other patients waiting to see doctors, and wished I could tell them I was really okay—imagining what it must be like to hear another patient screaming that way—but of course, I couldn't.

After hours of attempting to help me, the ER doctor eventually sent me to another hospital for an MRI, which proved inconclusive. For the next two weeks of our vacation, I spent all my time in a little bedroom downstairs in our Manzanita cabin while I waited to get better. The friends who owned the cabin allowed us to extend our time there so I could gear up for the trip home, but it became apparent that I would have to fly.

I spent part of the night before my flight soaking in a hot bath in a hotel near the airport. As the minutes of the night dragged on and the pain remained constant, I cried, I begged, I whimpered, I raged. Where was the loving support of Spirit in this experience? When I was wheeled on the plane the next morning I almost wept with gratitude. I was going home! Surely there I would begin to improve.

For the next month after returning home, I never slept more than ninety minutes at night. I was exhausted and began to experience real despair, as well as the fear that I would never be any better. During the long parade of interminable lonely nights, I counted the minutes until I could take my next dose of pain medication. In addition to medication, I tried all sorts of things to help reduce the pain: prayer, energy work, acupuncture, nutritional therapy, applications of mineral ice, chiropractic, repeated icing, lying on tobacco placed in a small flat bundle against the injured vertebrae for twenty minutes several times a day. Only deep muscle work by Peter Michael, a local pain-relief expert, made much impact. I had more tests performed during a stay in the hospital, all of which proved inconclusive. While everything helped a little, and a couple of things significantly reduced the pain temporarily, eventually I began to realize that no one could really do any more to help me get better. I had been waiting for these tests and therapists to "save me," and I was finally tired of it.

I decided I would take charge of the situation, and I began to do exercises for deeply hurt backs on my own. Slowly, I saw small amounts of improvement. I began physical therapy and then graduated to home exercise maintenance. I was finally getting better. It was February 7, my son's eighteenth birthday, almost seven months after the crisis in Manzanita.

Throughout the worst of this time, my greatest fear was that I would never improve. But I had a lot of time to reflect on other things that needed examining as well. For more than a year preceding my disability I had been aware that I wasn't handling the stress of my job at the church well. I had had numerous illnesses and injuries that seemed stress related: headaches, mouth sores, pneumonia, a previous back injury, an abnormal EKG. But I had continued at my frantic pace, thinking that I would just persevere until my son graduated from high school and the church got settled in a new home. But while flat on my back, I had to own up to the fact that I had been resisting an important inner message from the Divine Feminine for a long time. This message went deeper than the need to rest and replenish energy. I didn't want to know that I was being guided to release my life as I had known it. It frightened me even to consider it, pushing my trust in the Divine to the maximum of my capacity.

With no way to escape the truth through busyness, I had to admit what my inner wisdom was telling me: I had to leave the church and follow the path of the unknown before me. On February 1, I resigned my position. I had served as a senior minister in churches for twelve years and had been very active in my overall church organization. What I was to do now was unclear. I stepped into the void. I had no church, no position, no work. My body was broken. My son would soon graduate from high school and move out of state for college. The familiar roles with which I'd identified myself were falling away, leaving nothing to replace them. It was a profound experience of loss and brokenness.

It was also a great gift. In the surrender, I could look back and see how the Divine Feminine had been guiding me throughout this terrible darkness. Though it didn't eliminate my pain, it continued to reveal to me what I needed to know. Drawing the right healers and friends into my life at the right moment, directing me to the next healing step, it led me forward, helping me rebuild my life. My back improved greatly; my stress diminished. I moved to a beautiful, peaceful area in northern California and began to work on this book. I arrived here just in time to help a friend facing surgery and chemotherapy, something neither of us could have foreseen.

I am endlessly grateful for the healing of my body, but the real healing was in acknowledging that a new life was calling to me. I had new work to do, and in order to make myself available to do it, I had to release the life I knew. I'm not sure anything less than a forced stop would have empowered me to make that choice, but in the midst of involuntary immobility I experienced tremendous pain, fear, and despair. The sense of loss—of health, identity, income, and work—was profound.

Only once before had I experienced so profound a loss of identity, and that was when I was divorced. Divorce affects a huge number of people every year. As we take apart a relationship that began with shared dreams and promises, it isn't unusual to feel we no longer know who we are. We have identified ourselves as part of a couple, and our lives have become intertwined in our children, friends, memories, belongings, and schedules. Tearing apart the fabric of those intertwined lives is painful at best and terribly disorienting at worst. On the album, *Cry Like a Rainstorm, Howl Like the Wind,* Linda Ronstadt sings, "Shattered, like a window pain broken by a stone, each tiny piece of me lies alone and scattered." The lyric is a good description of the divorce experience for many people.

In the process of facilitating a divorce-recovery class, I learned even more about the power that divorce can have in a person's life. In taking apart the shared identity lies a dismantling, or breaking apart, of our own sense of self. Sometimes the loss of the dream of the family life we hoped we would have in the future is as painful as the loss of the relationship itself.

The day my husband and I decided to divorce after ten years of marriage, I remember sitting in the living room of our house in the rocking chair where I had spent so many hours nursing and rocking our son as an infant. It was a gorgeous, sunny September day in Seattle. The weather seemed to be mocking me. I couldn't understand how life could go on as if nothing had happened, when the universe was shattering within and around me.

Although I never identified the end of my marriage as a failure, the feelings of loss were so profound I truly felt like a bruised and beaten loser. I had lost my vision for the future. The Bible wisely says, "Where there is no vision, the people perish." In times of brokenness, we must find our way to a new vision for our lives. It takes time and energy, and we are fragile in this broken state, so progress is usually slow. We must be boundlessly gentle to ourselves in such times, for though the bruises we feel are usually emotional rather than physical, they are there all the same. Our resistance to disease tends to be lower during such crises, as well as our emotional resilience. We may be quick to anger or tears, unable to come to balance as we are accustomed to doing. Finding a new vision for the future means taking these temporary limitations into consideration and proceeding with patience and gentleness.

According to Dr. Bruce Fischer, who wrote the book *Rebuilding When Your Relationship Ends*, people feel depressed, angry, guilty, and a whole range of other emotions in the process of releasing a marriage. There's a story in Dr. Fischer's book about a woman who watched her ex-husband go into the mall with his new girlfriend. She rushed over and let the air out of all his tires, then she stayed hidden in the garage and waited to see his face when he returned to the car. Such things really do happen. Brad, one of the students in my class, told me with a sheepish smile that he had taken a pair of pliers and twisted the stems off his ex-wife's tires, rendering them both useless and irredeemable.

Anger is often part of our experience of working through the powerlessness our feelings of brokenness engender. Making plans to reclaim our lives by slowly involving ourselves in activities that seem interesting to us can help refocus our attention away from the anger and onto rebuilding. It is in this rebuilding that we discover talents and budding wisdom we hadn't recognized before. These are clues to the new vision for our future. It is here that the Divine Feminine helps reveal to us deeper parts of ourselves and how they can be included in the life in which we find ourselves in the wake of a breakdown. This rebuilding and discovery of newness in ourselves begins to work like the gold filigree cementing together the broken urn. While we can tell we've been broken, we also see new strength and beauty in ourselves.

While facilitating a WOMANSPIRIT retreat in northern California, I invited a woman named Judith to speak during one of our discussion sessions. In the context of some sharing we had been doing regarding motherhood, Judith spoke about the pain she still felt over the loss of a child she had given birth to as a teenager. Her mother had insisted she give the child up for adoption. Judith had not been able to conceive another child, and now, at middle age, she knew she never would. Although she was participating in raising her husband's two girls, Judith often wondered what had happened to her birth daughter. Her feelings touched all of us deeply. Just then, Carol, another retreat participant, stood and thanked Judith for allowing her child to be adopted. Carol was an adoptive mother who had been unable to conceive despite every effort and procedure. The anguish and feelings of frustration and failure due to her infertility had been compounded by a first adoption gone wrong, in which the birth mother had changed her mind and had come to reclaim the child. With the continued prompting of the Divine Feminine — that irresistible urge they felt within to be parents — Carol and her husband had gained the courage to try adopting again. Their beautiful child and the experience of parenting were a gift, Carol believed, from a mother who had been willing to give a child up. Carol embraced Judith with gratitude and comfort as the rest of us wiped tears from our eyes.

Both Judith and Carol had been immersed in the pain of loss regarding childbearing, but from different points of view. Embracing each other brought completion and resolution, in a small way, to both their stories. Those of us witnessing this exchange felt the hand of the Divine Feminine revealing to us all a truth we are not often privileged to see, namely, how both sides of the story can come together and reveal the gift that came out of the pain of those broken hearts.

Brokenness does need resolution. Just as a broken bone heals best after it has been set in proper alignment, so we heal best from our emotional brokenness and loss when we find our way to some sort of resolution. In Judith and Carol's case the resolution included personally sharing the story of someone on the opposite side of the experience that had broken each of them.

But we need not have another person against which to balance our own experience in order to come to resolution. Like my back crisis saga, there are times when the only real resolution is one we come to within ourselves, when we decide that things are going to change *now*. In order for our crisis to shift toward resolution, what has to change first is our attitude and our behavior. We begin to think about our situation in a new way and to respond to it according to the new thinking. This happened for me when I realized that no one and nothing outside me had the answer to my healing. If I was going to be well, it would be because of my own thoughts and actions. That was my turning point of power. Before that moment, I was at the mercy of doctors and healers, hopeful that they would find my answer. After that moment, I was in charge of the process that would bring me back to wholeness. The determination that came over me and pushed me into that power shift was the voice of the Divine Feminine within me, telling me to get up and take charge, to move on and regain my vision. The only person who can change the thoughts and actions we engage in is our self—the person who is shattered. Once we genuinely make that decision to change, the information we need to know or actions we need to take will reveal themselves.

For Andy, Luke, Judith, Carol, and myself, the Divine Feminine was always at work, though in the darkest part of our journeys it's unlikely any of us knew it. Somehow, though, we let that consoling presence of inner wisdom shine a light on the path out of the pain, and we followed the path. Each of us walked a path that led into the darkness, but it did not end there, as we had feared it might. Instead, as we followed the lead of the Divine Feminine, It took us to a place of increased brightness, hope, and vision. Judith was given the experiential understanding of how releasing her child for adoption might have stemmed the tide of pain in another woman's life. Carol was able to directly give thanks to a woman whose sacrifice had soothed the pain of childlessness, and in so doing, to help many women witness the devastating experience of infertility, cultivating their compassion. Andy discovered the everlasting arms of Spirit underlying his life, even at its most difficult and frightening, and he blossomed into greater trust and relaxation. Luke was blessed to be put into a position to test and witness his own courage. I found a new vision for my life as a writer and speaker that promises more balance and gentleness than the life I lived before my back crisis.

The poet William Stafford wrote, "I have woven a parachute out of everything broken." In every case of loss the directive of the Divine Feminine is to surrender and trust. The more we relive the brokenness, the more we revisit the grief, replaying the events that led up to it, the longer it takes us to discover what is being given to counterbalance the loss. If we are broken, we are not meant to remain that way. We are urged by the Divine Feminine to pay attention to the clues that are before us to lead us out of the darkness and into the new vision for our lives.

Sometimes it is only crisis that will motivate us to surrender to the newness of what we must become to be fully ourselves. A caterpillar must surrender its chrysalis to live the life of a butterfly. But we cannot help the butterfly as it struggles to emerge. If we do, it will die or never be capable of flight, for its efforts are designed to press the fluid out of its body and into its wings, balancing the butterfly's body and strengthening the wings so that they can lift the body in flight. Sometimes we think we'll be safer if we stay in our chrysalis, but if we want to fly, the chrysalis has got to go. And we must struggle to be born into the new life in order to gain the strength we need to live it well.

It is said that necessity is the mother of invention. When we have a choice between stagnating in pain or moving into a new vision of life and self, leaving the pain behind, which outcome do we really want?

In Zen Buddhist teachings, we read this story from *Zen Flesh, Zen Bones*, compiled by Paul Reps and Nyogen Senzaki:

Suiwo, the disciple of Hakuin, was a good teacher. During one summer seclusion period, a pupil came to him from a southern island of Japan.

Suiwo gave him the problem: "Hear the sound of one hand." The pupil remained three years, but could not pass this test. One night he came in tears to Suiwo. "I must return south in shame and embarrassment," he said, "for I cannot solve my problem."

"Wait one week more, and meditate constantly," advised Suiwo. Still no enlightenment came to the pupil. "Try for another week," said Suiwo. The pupil obeyed, but in vain. "Still another week." Yet this was of no avail.

In despair, the student begged to be released, but Suiwo requested another meditation of five days. They were without result. Then he said: "Meditate for three days longer, then if you fail to attain enlightenment, you had better kill yourself."

On the second day, the pupil was enlightened.

My students and congregants laugh when they hear this story, and I think it's because we can all recognize that sometimes we'd prefer to give up and go home to the past rather than have to do the really hard work it takes to move forward into the new life before us. But there is no going back, and there is nothing like a powerfully motivating deadline! Once we have been broken the only options are to live broken or to choose healing. In both cases life will never be what it was before. The good news is, choosing healing means it can be better.

Five

The Journey from Death to Rebirth

Do not stand at my grave and weep.
I am not there, I do not sleep.
I am a thousand winds that blow.
I am the diamond glint on snow.
I am the sunlight on ripened grain.
I am the gentle autumn rain.
When you wake in the morning hush
I am the swift uplifting rush
of quiet birds in circling flight.
I am the soft starlight at night.
Do not stand at my grave and cry.
I am not there. I did not die.

—*Author unknown*

Most of the sacred traditions of the world tell us that life doesn't end with the death of the physical body. We also have abundant testimonials from people who came close to death but were revived through medical or other interventions.

These folks relate similar experiences: seeing a bright light at the end of a dark tunnel through which they rapidly traveled; being greeted by a being or beings of light who asked them what they'd learned; being offered an opportunity to return to their lives in order to complete some work on the human plane. In some variations the dying person meets friends and relatives who have previously died. A small number of people tell frightening stories of what they saw, experienced, and interpreted as hell.

Personally, I feel that life goes on after the death of the physical body. Throughout my lifetime I have experienced the deaths of a number of family members and friends, yet I've often felt their presence and influence around me for some time after their funerals. As a minister, I have visited those grappling with life-threatening illnesses, and been present at a number of deaths, or transitions, as we refer to them in Religious Science. The dying and their family members have related communications and experiences to me that are difficult to interpret in our familiar fact-based, measurement-oriented medical model. As a result of all these experiences, my conviction regarding the ongoingness of life feels more like knowing than believing.

Death is probably the most mysterious of all our personal journeys. Every culture and religion throughout time has had its own special ways of preparing for and commemorating the deaths of family and community members. The death of someone we love is one of the most difficult experiences of darkness human beings face. We may have faith that helps sustain us and gives meaning to our experience, and this is very good. But the experience of loss and emptiness remains. We will not see that face, hear that voice, feel that touch, ever again. Even video and audiotape cannot convey the living, breathing presence of that person in the fullness we ache for so much. We must walk through the experience of loss by whatever path best suits our own personality and faith.

Death is the most final of all the changes we experience. I remember talking with a woman in northern California a year after the San Francisco earthquake in which one of the freeway bridges collapsed. A friend and co-worker of hers had been killed on the freeway that day. "I know it doesn't make sense," she told me, "but every day that he's gone, I get angrier. He's still dead! When is he going to get over it and come home?"

Letting go of a loved one and feeling the relentless ongoingness of his or her absence changes us. Yet never at any point on our human journey of evolution—even in facing death—are we immune to the encouragement of the Divine Feminine to learn from our experiences. A friend of mine used to call this the divine economy of God, that even our painful moments in life are not wasted but become opportunities to choose to expand ourselves in love and strength. Facing death—our own, or that of someone we love—is certainly one of these.

As long as my mother was alive, somewhere in the back of

my mind I knew that I always had a place to go if things in my life ever fell apart. After she died, it slowly dawned on me that it was my responsibility, and only mine, to take care of myself. Although I was thirty-seven years old at the time, I felt like an orphan. I had a sense of being on the front line even though I still had aunts and uncles. Somehow my mother's death signaled the end of an era of my life. There was no longer anyone in front to lead the way, even figuratively, anymore. Now it was up to me.

Shortly after my mother died, I had a dream in which I was walking up a grassy hill, and suddenly she was there with me, walking too. She was wearing her usual beige raincoat, and looked entirely like herself, tiny and fragile. I was overjoyed to see her, knowing full well in the dream that she was dead, and I asked if I could take a picture of her. "Is that allowed?" I asked. "Yes," she said, "it's allowed." "I have pictures of you before death; this will be a picture *after* death," I said, preparing to take the photo. But before I could get the camera to my eye, Mom stepped forward and took my face gently in her hands. Looking lovingly into my eyes, she said, "I am all right. I just want you to know, I am all right." That was the end of the dream. I never got my photo, but the dream helped me with my feelings of grief, as well as serving as a confirmation of my own faith about the continuation of life.

From the spiritual perspective, our life does not begin with birth nor does it end with death. The Divine Feminine, in addition to being an aspect of the Creator, is a part of us that isn't bound by time, space, or form. Its dimension of existence enfolds life on earth, but exists beyond it as well. The body serves us throughout our lives as a temple of our Spirit. With this awareness, at the time of physical death, the body should be honored by our loved ones for having housed our Spirit during our life on earth. Nevertheless, the body isn't needed when we move on to the next expression of life any more than it was needed before we came into the world, so we lay it down and go on.

I've been honored to sit with the dying and their families as they prepared for the transition to come, and I've been challenged by the grief of those whose loved ones have died suddenly, as well as the emptiness of those left behind who have no belief in the continuity of life. I've seen the difference between the experience of those who were traversing the space from one world to the next, and those who could only watch them go. While parts of these two experiences of death overlap, they are also distinct in their demands on the people who are in the midst of them. I'd like to say that all of the dying who have time to prepare themselves for the coming transition make peace with the process before the final moment, but not everyone does. I'd like to say that families always pull together, putting aside old family grudges and hurts to support one another, but not all of them can. There are those, however, who seem to understand in a special way what is happening to them or to their loved one. These people and their way of coming to death are instructive to all of us. We can learn something from them about the process that can bring increased peace to our own experiences of death.

One point of view about death holds that our lives continue until we have finished our task here on earth, no matter how long or short the life or the manner of the death. I experienced this view when a special family in northern California asked me to facilitate the memorial service for their seven-year-old daughter, Suzanna.

Suzanna had been playing in a field during a large family birthday party and had wandered too close to the bordering road. She was hit by a car and killed instantly. As we planned her memorial, Suzanna's parents told me that they fully understood, in retrospect, that it had been time for Suzanna to go. Looking back on her short life, her parents saw that Suzanna had been a marvel of wisdom and love for them and for her older brother. Many gifts had been given and lessons learned from their short time together. Although their grief was deep and profound, Suzanna's family sent her off into the next life with celebration and gratitude. They held no rancor for the driver of the car, knowing that person had had no warning before the child appeared. From her parents' perspective, Suzanna had, on some level of consciousness, *chosen* to go during a celebration, not realizing it would bring sadness to those in attendance but feeling it would be a perfect time, leaving everyone in love and laughter.

Perhaps this seems like an elaborate coping mechanism, but whatever it is, it was deeply real and true for this family.

Their beliefs about Suzanna's death bonded them closely with one another, gave meaning to their grieving, and opened their hearts to others who had lost children. The Divine Feminine touched them through their pain, and they responded. Their loving courage inspired friends who even today continue to talk about that special memorial service.

When I discuss death with my students in spiritual classes, I find that those who have lost a loved one to death often have a depth not yet present in those who have never experienced such loss, no matter what their ages. There is a maturing and compassion that can come from bearing the pain of a beloved person's death. Some people express an absolute conviction that life continues after physical death as a result of their experience. Others aren't sure of anything except the vital importance of the support of friends and family members during the grieving time, and because they know this, they are often better equipped to comfort others who are grieving.

There are times when we cannot prepare for death, when it comes into our lives suddenly and roughly. Allen and Sally were the devoted parents of four adult children, two girls and two boys. Death hit them terribly hard when both their daughters committed suicide in the same year. The elder daughter had struggled for years with a drug addiction that began when she was a junior in high school. The second daughter had been dealing with mental illness and finally lost her battle. The pain of losing two children in this terrible way left the parents in more than shock. The anguished question *why*—a question we can never answer in a way that provides satisfaction—filled their nights and days.

We planned another memorial after the death of the second daughter. Family and friends who had come together once before returned to comfort Sally and Allen and share their grief again. The darkness was almost unbearable. Yet family members believed that both young women were now free of the imprisonment they knew no way to endure. Sally and Allen did what they could to bless both daughters on their way in God's love and to leave what they couldn't understand in God's care. Some time later their eldest son married, and all of us came together yet again, but this time in celebration.

Life is seasonal and cyclical. It doesn't begin and end; it flows endlessly from birth, through life, to death, and on to rebirth and new life. Our grief at endings is a necessary part of the cycle. It helps us to recognize we must go on into the new cycle, though we may feel crushed and empty ourselves. Just as many of the growing things of earth appear to be dead in the winter, then bloom in opulent beauty in the spring, so we occasionally experience a winter of the soul when we must become quiet and introspective. It is a time for stillness and waiting. Spring does return. We will be refreshed and "reborn." The simple recognition that spring always comes can help comfort us as it reminds us of the possibility that those we love continue to exist in a new springtime somewhere beyond our sight and understanding.

The time of stillness and waiting is easier when we know

this and allow it than when we try to keep ourselves always in the spring and summer of life. There are hard winters and mild winters, long winters and short winters, but there are no permanent winters. An engraving that appears on the New England headstone of Herry Scott Holland, 1847–1918, canon of St. Paul's Cathedral, reveals this sentiment:

What is Death? Death is nothing at all. I have only slipped away into the next room. I am I and you are you. Whatever we were to each other, that we are still. Call me by my old familiar name. Speak to me in the easy way you always used to. Put no difference in your tone. Wear no forced air of solemnity or sorrow. Laugh as we always laughed at the little jokes we enjoyed together. Play, smile, think of me, pray for me. Let my name be ever the household word that it always was. Let it be spoken without effect, without the trace of a shadow on it. Life means all that it ever meant. It is the same that it ever was. There is absolutely unbroken continuity. Why should I be out of mind because I am out of sight? I am waiting for you, for an interval, somewhere very near, just around the corner. All is well.

The challenge of releasing a loved one in death is especially difficult when the death is sudden or untimely. We may feel as if the aliveness in us died with that person and we are merely walking zombies, alive in form but not in spirit. Yet, as alone as we feel, the Divine Feminine surrounds and enfolds us.

The Divine Feminine enters the very place where we cannot understand what is happening or why. Grieving a death obviously cannot fill the void left by the person who has died, but grieving can deepen our compassion and stir us to take on some of the family roles left behind by our loved one. Ultimately it is the ongoingness of our own life—which we experience as the days and weeks stretch onward after the death of a loved one—that brings us healing and comfort.

In cases where death is foreseen, rather than sudden, and the one dying is aware of what is happening, death can bring with it a unique willingness to heal relationships and leave life in a greater state of peace than one may have lived during most of it. Death can become, for some, an opportunity to experience, in a broader perspective, the meaning of life. I believe this opportunity is the energy of the Divine Feminine pressing onward, never giving up on us in its mission to awaken us to full awareness.

Sam was a longtime friend of mine from Seattle. Sam's partner, Paul, is a deeply spiritual man of faith, although Sam himself was not. One day when Paul returned from shopping, Sam eagerly announced he'd had a visitor in Paul's absence: "an energy of light and love and movement," he said. "Oh, you're just saying that to make me feel better," Paul chided, feeling Sam was trying to embrace a spiritual possibility he didn't really feel to provide some comfort to the devout partner who would be left alone so soon. "No, no," Sam assured him fervently, "it really happened!" He referred to the visitor as "my friend" in several subsequent conversations, reporting other visits.

Sam's condition continued to worsen until he was struggling through his last few breaths several weeks later. Suddenly he brightened, and said, "I'm at the train station! And there's my friend! He's holding his hand out to me, saying, 'Come on, it's time to go . . .' " With that, Sam lifted his hand toward his vision, closed his eyes, and died. Paul told me later that his own belief in life after death, and the support we all have as we make that life transition, has grown stronger through his experience with Sam.

People experiencing illness or old age who are preparing themselves for death sometimes begin to see and hear things that those around them do not. Medical professionals will sometimes attribute this to medication, dementia, or the chemical changes in the brain that precede death, yet the vast spectrum of documented cases of the near-death experience, covering such a variety of states and conditions, brings reasonable doubt to these theories. I prefer to think of such visions as the time when the veil between the worlds—between the sensory human experience on earth and the spiritual life that follows—becomes thin, and we spend a bit of time in both places, preparing ourselves for the final passing into the new realm. There is certainly more to this process of death than we can yet explain. Perhaps it is too easy to assume that Sam saw into his own future in nonphysical reality, but we have no proof to indicate he did not.

One's own death is a journey that is ultimately made alone, no matter what our position in society or the number of people we have to love and support us. For a person facing death there are many things to think about: his will; what he wants done at his memorial; how to face the emotional and frightening prospect of letting go of life and loved people and things so permanently; how to bring completion to relationships that need attention.

Frank, who lived in northern California, was diagnosed with terminal cancer. He had never been to our church, nor had his wife, Marion, but she had a friend who attended. Near the end of his life, Frank began to explore what might be on the other side of death, and Marion asked me to come and speak with him.

Frank's family of origin was of stoic German stock, not religiously or emotionally inclined, and the continuity of life had never been a topic of conversation among them. He and I talked for about an hour considering what might follow death. Frank's point of view was unformed and he was hungry for information to consider. I was honored to share my thoughts and beliefs with him.

At the end of our talk Frank said to me, "I've talked to all my brothers and sisters, and my kids and Marion know I love them. The only person I haven't talked to is my mother. I just don't know what to say to her." I paused, then said, "Perhaps it doesn't matter *what* you say. It's enough just to let her know you love her and you're sorry to be leaving her. It may not seem like much now, but it will be very important to her after you're gone." Marion told me that later that day Frank telephoned his mother and they spoke for quite a while. I don't know what was said, but not long after that, he went on to the next plane of life.

Some days after Frank's memorial service Marion told me she felt angry that his family had missed out on knowing this wonderful man during the years that Frank had been healthy. He had been gruff—the strong, silent type. In earlier times of minor illness Frank had behaved like a fussy child, constantly complaining and criticizing any attempts to help him. His teenaged children had never met the loving, patient man inside until after his cancer diagnosis.

Marion was grieving what the children had missed during those early years, but without the trauma of a terminal illness, Frank might never have discovered that part of himself. None of his family members would have known what they'd missed. Frank's cancer helped him ripen to the change that was next for him, both in terms of his life's transition and of the opening of his heart. Perhaps it was the only thing that would have allowed him to do so.

What comes after death is a subject of much speculation. What we choose to believe often comes down to our culture and faith. I see death as another kind of birth. Before our birth, in utero, our total concept of life is the one within the womb. Once born and in the midst of our life on earth, we resemble the unborn child, safe in what she knows. We, too, think we know what life is. What lies beyond this life experience is unknown to us so far, like the mapmakers of the Middle Ages who drew dragons and drop-offs at the end of the familiar, explored geography. Yet I believe we will find friends and loving hands waiting to welcome us as we pass to the next expression of life from this one. I believe that the life that follows physical death is another aspect of the seasons. As we enter this new realm of existence, the Divine Feminine guides us into the unknown safely and lovingly, becoming the midwife to whom we finally surrender ourselves as we let go of the familiar and move on.

Chris, a dear friend who was experiencing AIDS-related health complications, had asked me what I thought life after death was like. Several people who were close to us had died that year, and he remarked that many of them were artists, as he was. "Maybe something *big* is about to happen on the other side and all of them are needed now," he said. Always the prima donna, he joked, "I wouldn't mind being there, too, as long as I could make a lot of the decisions!" We laughed. I remembered the following story, which I then shared with Chris:

Ram Dass, the former Harvard psychology professor famous for LSD experiments in the 1960s who later became a student of Eastern philosophies and a much-sought-after author, speaker, and workshop leader, asked Emmanuel, one of his spiritual teachers, "Emmanuel, what should I tell people about death?" And Emmanuel answered, "Tell them it's perfectly safe. Tell them it's like taking off a tight shoe. It's like being at a party where a lot of people are talking and smoking, and stepping outside for a breath of fresh air." This story always brings me a sense of peace. I hope that in the lonely moments when Chris faced that unknown, these thoughts gave him comfort, too.

Several months later Chris was surrounded in the hospital with friends and relatives who kept a vigil in his room as we waited for his transition. We honored his request to fill the room with music and light as we played tapes and told stories of our experiences with him. We shared a lot of laughter, prayer, and some tears as Chris's condition deteriorated and he entered a coma. I will always remember his words on the last day he was really lucid. He spoke to each person in the circle surrounding him in his hospital bed, telling each of us what we meant to him and thanking us for being part of his life. Then he said, "Even though I know that death is near, I don't feel afraid because I have all of you here with me." He died peacefully a few days later on Easter Sunday.

Death humbles us, because we cannot overcome it. It overpowers us—we certainly cannot control it. What we can do is witness death respectfully, and preserve as much dignity as we are able for our loved ones who are passing. Sometimes this is difficult when our loved one is already in the hospital. Traditional medicine is dedicated to supporting life at all costs, and sometimes that cost is the dignity of those we love. We do not have a culture that remembers how to honor death as a part of life; we view it as something gone wrong, even when the dying person has lived a long, full life.

Rose was past ninety when she was admitted to the hospital. As I visited her there, the discharge nurse came in to discuss plans for Rose's possible release from the medical center, which resulted in a rather humorous conversation from my standpoint as an observer. When the nurse asked Rose if she had help at home, Rose replied, "Yes, I have someone who comes to clean and do the laundry, and someone who helps me wash my hair." Noting that Rose wouldn't be able to return to the apartment where she'd lived alone, the nurse asked Rose where she planned to go. "Well, either I'll get well enough to go home or I'll make my transition," Rose replied. "And what will that be?" the nurse asked. Rose tried again. "You know, I'll either get well or go on to my next experience." "Yes, and what is your plan for that next experience?" the nurse prompted again. Rose sighed in exasperation, looked at me, then said to the nurse, "This is my minister." Turning to me, she said, *"You* tell her!" "Rose is saying that either she'll get well or she'll die," I said simply. The nurse became flustered and responded, "Oh! I'm sure there is something between those two extremes!" In answer, Rose fixed the nurse with a sharp, perplexed look, and asked, "Do you realize that I'm ninety-one?"

To Rose, her coming death was a natural part of life. She felt no fear or resistance at the prospect of leaving her body. But to the nurse it represented a possible failure on the part of the medical system itself, and it was up to her to prevent it as long as possible, never mind that Rose was ninety-one and ready to go.

Death is the great common denominator. Every day we practice how we will face it as we are confronted with the need to let go of little things to which we feel attached. Jobs evolve, bodies change, children grow up and start their own lives. Moment by moment we face death. Our grief is an important part of releasing things large and small. When we let the grief wash over and through us for those we have lost in death, we soften and become more compassionate. We understand better the fragile, priceless quality of a human life, and in this we may discover more tenderness and compassion for our own foibles and those of others around us.

The only way to come to the end of the sadness is to go through it. If we try to postpone our grieving, it comes back to us later in full force. We really do need a great deal of emotional support and understanding in times of grief. That is why various agencies and organizations provide survivor support groups for spouses, partners, children, parents, siblings, and friends whose loved ones have died. There is nothing like being with people who have experienced what you are going through to provide meaningful comfort. As much as others who care about us may listen to our tears and encourage our healing, without the shared experience they are unable to really meet our sadness. If you are experiencing the death of a loved one, I encourage you to find a group in your area to attend with others who have had similar experiences. Their listening and understanding is a soothing balm that can help us go on. As a synergistic, holistic energy, the Divine Feminine often reveals Itself in the dynamic of a group. The sharing of common feelings and experiences brings forth truths we can't get to alone when we're struggling to figure things out intellectually. The Divine Feminine is not only the midwife that births us into the new life but is also the presence of comfort and peace that can come upon us in the time of deep grief after the death of a loved one.

When we listen to It, it is the Divine Feminine that helps us realize that there is indeed more to life and reality than we can see and understand with our intellect. As the Fox tells the Prince in Antoine de St. Exupéry's story, *The Little Prince,* "It is only with the heart that one can see rightly. What is essential is invisible to the eye."

This common funeral reading, by an unknown author, summarizes the comforting idea that the life of one who has left his or her physical body continues—somewhere ever so slightly beyond our range of vision and comprehension:

I am standing upon the seashore. A ship at my side spreads her white sails to the morning breeze and starts for the blue ocean. She is an object of beauty and strength, and I stand and watch her until at length she hangs like a speck of white cloud, just where the sea and sky come together to mingle with each other.

Then someone at my side says, "There! She's gone!" Gone where? Gone from my sight, that's all. She is just as large in mast and hull and span as she was when she left my sight, and she is just as able to bear her load of living weight to her destined port. Her diminishing size is in me, not in her, and just at the moment when someone at my side says, "There! She's gone!" there are other eyes watching her coming and other voices taking up the glad shout, "Here she comes!"—and that is dying. There is no death.

For years after my mother died, things she would have found funny stimulated an impulse in me to go to the phone and call her to share the joke. Within a moment, of course, I realized this was something I couldn't do. This familiar impulse eventually faded, and occurs only rarely now. Yet as I grow older, I find there is a richness in remembering my mother and what she enjoyed. I recognize it as a part of the tapestry of my own life, my memories, my joys. When little reminders of her occur, rather than bringing sadness they now leave me with a feeling of warmth and appreciation for the life we shared.

As family members and friends, we can honor the dying process and all the confusing feelings around it by simply being present with the dying person and remaining aware of our feelings. If that person wants to talk about what is happening, our job is to listen fully first, then respond if we have anything to say. It is not necessary to have words of wisdom. Just being there is enough. If the dying person is quiet, honoring her process may lead us to be quiet with her.

When we finally face our own death we will choose the life

message we leave with our loved ones by how we handle our dying process. We will have learned something about this from everyone we have known whose death has touched us. If we cultivate a willingness to gather information and grow in awareness, there is a better chance we will have the courage to share our love and appreciation with those who remain behind when our time comes to go. We will be better equipped to share our thoughts and feelings with them and to encourage them to share theirs with us. As we learn how to let go now, there is more likelihood that we will go gently and peacefully into the realm of tomorrow, with a sense of completion to a life well-lived, eager and able to join the friends who wait for us beyond the veil.

Part Two

QUALITIES
OF BEING

Six

Qualities of Being
and Guidance

....

At each stage of learning, we must give up something, even if
it is a way of life that we have always known.

—*Ginevee, Australian aboriginal,*
quoted by Lynn Andrews in Crystal Woman

Qualities of Being are ways of focusing our attitudes and
actions to maximize benefit from all our life experiences, particularly our experiences of darkness. Learning to utilize these
Qualities is a way of becoming aware of, opening more fully to,
and cooperating with the Guidance actively exists within us at
all times. In fact, these Qualities can help us move successfully
through the dark, challenging times of our lives, as well as liv-

ing our daily lives more peacefully. Each of the Qualities of Being has two components: attitude and action. Practicing the Qualities is like being on a journey toward spiritual maturity, a journey in which certain tasks must be successfully completed in order to gain tools to empower one further along the way. Life challenges catapult us into this journey, but rather than being physical, the tasks we are asked to accomplish to mature spiritually are internal. At the gateway to each new stage of development, an angel sentinel stands in the midst of our darkness, and says, "You must let go first." In order to utilize the tools of the Qualities of Being, we must let go of the attitudes that can block their effectiveness. Each stage on the journey toward spiritual maturity requires its own letting go.

Imagine there is an angel waiting in the darkness of your challenge who is a guardian at the entry to a passageway that leads through the darkness to the light. In order for you to enter and successfully move through the passageway, you need the angel's help and Guidance. The angel requires that you leave behind that which has thus far hindered you—an old familiar attitude—before you can enter the passageway. The angel then gives you a tool to help you through that passageway, an empowering gift of one of the Qualities of Being: attention, intention, choice, practice, surrender, intuition, gratitude, or trust. You must actively use the Quality of Being the angel has given you in order to continue to progress through the passageway. The passage may be long or short; there is no way of knowing in advance. But if you faithfully use the Quality of Being you have been given, you will emerge into the light at the other end of the passageway with some new awareness. This new awareness will enrich your life in ways you never imagined before the time of darkness began. Each Quality of Being works this way. By their very nature, the Qualities increase our experience of light.

Of course, the angel in the passageway is only a metaphor. It is a useful one, though, for understanding the way in which we must change our attitudes and behavior in order to come through a time of darkness with new awareness and strength.

Before examining the Qualities individually, it may be helpful to say more about Guidance itself, to clarify what it is and how it comes to us. The first time I recall encountering Guidance from the Divine Feminine I was in search of wisdom to make a difficult decision. I was a senior in high school and needed to decide whether to attend the public university or a private Catholic college that had offered me a scholarship. My family wanted me to attend the latter, as I had attended small Catholic elementary and high schools. They were concerned that I'd just get lost in the immense university system. I wasn't sure.

I had gone to the ocean with my senior class for a retreat. Being at the ocean was a precious experience for me. Growing up on Puget Sound in Seattle, I was accustomed to the sea, with all its wonderful moods and smells and colors, but to look out on that vast vista of power that is the Pacific with no land masses in sight was awesome.

Walking alone on the beach during quiet, private time I was, once again, pondering the question of where I should go to school. I couldn't sort it out and felt pulled both ways. I walked a long time in the fog on that beach, and by the time I turned around to walk back to the retreat center, I knew.

I never actively decided, I just knew. I was going to the University of Washington. There was no doubt in my mind, nor did I doubt at all that this was the right choice for me. I felt no qualms, then or at any time after that, about going forward with the arrangements to go there. And, as things turned out, not only did I not get lost in the crowd there, I thrived.

I knew at the time this happened to me that the experience was unusual. I had met the Divine Feminine in that nonlinear knowing for the first time. Now I would call what I experienced that day on the beach Guidance, but at the time I had no name for it, I just knew that I knew.

I believe there is an intuitive knowing within us that is always present. That knowing provides wisdom and insight to apply to the circumstances of our lives as they arise, and is always perfectly tailored to us and our situation. It is the voice of the Divine Feminine, an aspect of the presence of Spirit within us at all times, and also outside of and beyond us. Guidance is always present; our receptivity, however, is variable. A radio that is carelessly set will produce static all day. Such static never bothers the radio. The radio will continue in that way until the tuning is adjusted to capture the station signal clearly, and then the information or music can be heard and enjoyed.

Our consciousness works in a similar way. Unless we choose to give ourselves time to listen for Guidance we may feel confused and pressed by life, always overwhelmed and short of enthusiasm. Listening for Guidance allows us to tune in to the station properly. It reduces the effort involved in accomplishing tasks because we are no longer casting about aimlessly trying everything to find solutions. When we let Guidance provide insight before we act, we enter into focused clarity. We can go directly to the right action and do it. In the long run the overall time spent in an action will be less than that spent in the try-everything mode, but at the beginning there is much more of what appears to be doing nothing.

It is said that when the student is ready the teacher appears. With Guidance it seems that when an individual is ready to do less, to surrender, and to listen more with real openness and receptivity, Guidance occurs. Sometimes a person is at the end of his rope before he can let go and listen. Others make this listening part of their daily lives, releasing their own agendas and trusting the inner wisdom.

It is a matter of interest to me that a number of famous artists gave credit for their creations to a knowing that came from beyond themselves. Mozart said his compositions were the result of writing down what he heard. It wasn't a matter of being more educated, talented, or holy—from his perspective, he was taking dictation. He was "tuned in" to the right station for him and receptively responding. Michelangelo said he knew that the David was already in the marble. His job was to chip away the marble that did not belong there, so that the David could be revealed. Toscanini gave credit to God as the source of his work. To me, these are all examples of the inner knowing to which I'm referring—in each of these cases, the particular artist's Guidance in action.

Guidance is also plentiful in business, sports, and finance. *Vision* and *mission* are buzz words now in corporate culture. A company is told it needs to have a vision and a mission to guide its goals and objectives and against which to measure its success. But where does such a vision come from? It may result in part from gathering information and keeping in mind what the company does, but something else enters into the process that makes an effective corporate vision alive and electric in its ability to inspire and motivate.

In Robert Fritz's book *The Leader as Creator,* he addresses the process of creating a vision in this way:

> [E]very professional creator either consciously or intuitively thoroughly understands the principle of how a creator conceives of a vision. *The creator simply makes up the vision.*
>
> . . . Years ago I consulted with an engineering group in a high-tech organization. When I mentioned to the engineers this insight about the creative process, at first they looked at each other with knowing grins. Then one engineer after another said, "That's exactly what we do. We make up what we create." One of them added, "But then we

have to write technical articles explaining how we made it up in such a way that it doesn't seem made up.

The engineers Fritz consulted make up what they want to create. But what was the source of their made-up ideas? All creative ideas, it seems to me, exist within the boundless Mind of God. All these examples of ideas acted upon—Mozart, Michelangelo, the engineers in Fritz's story—are Guidance at work: the response of the Divine Feminine within to a specific challenge or problem.

Almost all of us have the experience of moments of insight—brilliant flashes of wisdom that come through us but don't seem to come from us. We can become more and more receptive to those flashes, letting them through without censoring or judging. This is not wisdom we can explain. It is nonlinear knowing, which bypasses the intellect. It is trustworthy. Sometimes it feels as if we just "made it up," and we discount it because we cannot "show our work." How did we know, how did we reach that conclusion? *We don't know how,* we just know. In their book, *If It Ain't Broke ... Break It!,* Robert Kriegel and Louis Patler point out that Martin Luther King, Jr., said, "I have a dream," he didn't say, "I have a strategic plan."

We can expand our receptivity to nonlinear knowing by experimenting in seeking Guidance while trusting that the Guidance is there for us. Without a willingness to expand our trust, the motivation to wait patiently, in spite of a feeling of urgency to act, will never materialize. Waiting is an essential part of receiving Guidance. Waiting requires a particular attitude of optimism, openness, and receptivity. To anyone who's spent hours waiting in line or on hold, it may seem surprising to know that waiting is an active rather than a passive process. Waiting for Guidance occurs with attention and intention, the first two Qualities of Being we will explore. A person trusts that Guidance is available and watches for it without preconceived ideas as to what it will look like and what it will require when it arrives.

Rev. Virginia Saville, a mentor of mine, says, "It isn't that God doesn't answer our prayers, it's that sometimes we don't like the answers!" She would go on to relate this example: A person prays to God, "Show me where I should live, God, a place where I will be happy and able to follow my dreams, a place where I will thrive and find fulfillment while serving others." And the answer within comes back, "Alaska." So the person prays again, "Please God, reveal to me where I should live, for my greatest happiness, and where what I do will make a difference to others." And the answer comes back a second time, "Alaska." So the person prays a third time. . . .

It can be easy to overlook the Guidance given to us when we have predetermined how a project or situation "has to go," because then we are only looking for what validates our preconception. If the answer is in a different direction from what we expected, we can mistake it for a distraction, or fail to notice it completely, while we continue to look for the recognizable response we've determined we must have. When that response doesn't show up, we claim that the Infinite doesn't provide Guidance or respond to our prayers. But this is never the case.

Being open to real Guidance allows the Universe to draw from infinite possibilities to respond to our situation. Being open to only a selected few options limits what the Universe can bring to our awareness and also limits what we can accomplish. Complete receptivity will often result in directions we couldn't have imagined and wouldn't have chosen on our own, yet these bring the most fulfilling and successful experiences.

On the road to spiritual maturity we discover again and again what we don't know. Each time a challenge arises in our life the choice is ours: will we try to control and force the situation, or will we relax and remain open to Guidance? This is particularly tricky in situations arising from circumstances to which we are well accustomed: a profession we've worked in for a long time, a long-term relationship. As our confidence in the familiar grows, our listening may diminish. We feel less need for insight or advice. We think we know everything about the work or about our partner. Watch out! Once we "know how" we stop creating and growing and we enter maintenance mode. This is useful for a time and is a part of the normal cycle of creation and re-creation, but we are not intended to remain in maintenance permanently. Lingering overlong we begin to stagnate, and so does the work or the relationship.

Qualities of Being

These are the Qualities of Being: *attention, intention, choice, practice, surrender, intuition, gratitude,* and *trust.* Each of these qualities relates in a special way to the Divine Feminine. Each one, when practiced, requires that we give up some old habit of being in order to make room for this new way of approaching our life. Each one also results in a new strength or gift in our lives once we begin to use it consistently. Each Quality has the ability to make our journey through times of darkness more meaningful and less frightening and painful,

	Divine Feminine Expresses As	*Must Release*
Attention	awareness of present moment nourished by the richness of all that is happening around us and all we see and experience right now	past/future focus guilt/anxiety
Intention	organic responses to demands of the moment while flowing gracefully with the unexpected	need for predictable or guaranteed outcomes; quitting when things don't go our way
Choice	honest, open, full disclosure of all issues, desires, and observations seeking win/win for all involved	identifying oneself as a victim
Practice	consistent, repeated, conscious action, while appreciating and savoring the process of unfoldment—no hurry	demand for instant results

and to make everyday life richer and more peaceful. Nothing will completely eliminate difficult emotions during the dark times (that's why we experience them as dark); nevertheless, using these Qualities of Being—these ways of interpreting our experiences, these habits of responding to the world—goes a long way toward helping us respond effectively and with balance when crisis hits and the familiar disappears.

To Gain	Crisis Benefit
present moment awareness	ability to stay in present time and respond in the now moment, minimizing influences from other times/places/people that are not part of the current challenge
richer vision and trust in God	allows us to stay involved and active with what is happening, while trusting the activity of God in each moment
empowerment	gives us back our dignity and confidence in our ability to know what we want and to choose it wisely, responsibly, and fairly
mastery	creates a foundation of stability and knowledge to rely upon during a challenge—a cushion of mental/physical/spiritual preparation and resilience

Divine Feminine Expresses As		*Must Release*
Surrender	letting go into the moment completely with abandon and trust, knowing all is always well	the need to be right, judging others
Intuition	an inner, nonlinear knowing—not derived from observable facts and conditions—which is life-expanding and enhancing	knowing it all already, "expert" consciousness, guarantee of being right before taking action
Gratitude	appreciation for the beauty that surrounds us, the good we already have in our lives, and the way in which we are constantly supported by the Universe	craving for more, taking things for granted
Trust	complete safety and ability to let go and creatively express all that is within us without fear	the need to understand

In stagnation, what worked before may stop working. This can be painful: we enter the darkness and wonder what's wrong. "Should I quit? Should I leave?" This painful wondering is a clue to move back into a receptive mode and ask for Guidance.

How does one go about seeking Guidance? Taking time for oneself is essential. In our busy, hectic lives it is common

To Gain	Crisis Benefit
safety and revelation	opens us to the Guidance that responds specifically to our need—trains us to respond to the clues we receive without having to know and understand everything about them
deep, true Guidance	direction can arise to assist us in knowing exactly what to do when there is no outward way we could have that information—we feel such deep certainty and recognition that we need no additional motivation to act
receiving and grace	brings our attention to the gifts we already possess and allows us to truly receive them and let them serve us
freedom	to let go into the flow of God knowing the activity of God is unfolding perfectly, whether we understand it or not

to not know what we think, feel, or want. Overwhelmed by everyday life, we may become so numb that we seem to have no thoughts, feelings, or desires. Honoring oneself by taking daily quiet time to think, write, and meditate begins to gently awaken us to ourselves. By waiting on our own thoughts and feelings and providing a safe place to feel and express them, we begin to rediscover what they are and, at an even deeper level, who we are as unique individuals.

This is profound. Guidance cannot come unless there is someone present there to receive it. Quiet time to think and reflect reveals to us how we really experience our lives and what we really want. Only then do we know which areas in our lives are in need of Guidance. Only then can we practice openness to listening and watching for it.

There is a secondary benefit to following Guidance into the unknown. It almost always reveals to us a new strength of character or reinforces a known strength in ways beyond what we considered ourselves capable of achieving. This new or increased strength prepares us, albeit unknowingly, for the opportunities coming up later on our path of unfoldment. We are better able to respond to these opportunities with resilience, courage, and joy because of the wisdom and strength we have gained in the practice of following Guidance and learning to trust it. Each time we follow the Guidance we are given, we are able to do so sooner and with more conviction the next time. As with everything, practice makes us stronger.

Guidance and the process of waiting for it are expressions of the Divine Feminine. Intuitive knowing emerging from the unknown, the pool of Infinite consciousness, is the Divine Feminine flowing through us. This very act of allowing the flow *through* us is the action of the Divine Feminine in form *as* us. Not only are we connected to this responsive aspect of the Universe, we are made from it and designed to use it. We do so naturally when we are relaxed, patient, and trusting.

When we are actively living this way and a crisis occurs, it is easier to apply our practice to the new experience. If practicing the Qualities of Being is new, crisis can jar us so completely we hardly know what to think or do. In the latter instance, it is helpful to think of the metaphor of the angel sentinels in the darkness who are there specifically for the purpose of helping us grow into greater awareness and strength.

I've heard that in Chinese the character for *crisis* is composed of two figures: danger and opportunity. The idea that every crisis is composed of both elements is a worthy one to consider. We see how danger works with opportunity in many areas of life. In investing, the higher the risk, the higher the interest or income available from the investment if it does come through. In medical research new technologies and drugs must be tested. Each test is a risk — perhaps a life-threatening one — to the animal or patient being used for the test, yet if the new development is successful, the animal or patient will be cured of the illness being studied. In space exploration each launch is, in part, a new development. The astronauts participating will be doing something for the first time. If their flight goes well, its results may bring the entire space program forward. If the flight fails people may lose their lives.

For most of us the crises we face rarely hold such huge possibilities for gain against the balance of our very lives. Our dangerous opportunities may be more like those we have explored in previous chapters. The risk to forgive, for example, has us balancing being rejected and feeling hurt once again, versus rebuilding a relationship or reclaiming personal peace. We don't know before making the attempt at forgiveness which of these will be the result of the effort. We must decide whether we will attempt forgiveness without that information.

As we learn about each Quality of Being, we can envision ourselves handing to the angels in the passageways each of the old attitudes that need releasing, and receiving instead a new Quality for practice. In practicing, we will be developing our own special skills and timing so that we will be prepared to live fully and freely and to respond wisely when a "dangerous opportunity" appears.

Seven

Attention

....

Truly it is in the darkness that one finds the light, so when we are in sorrow, then this light is nearest of all to us.

—Meister Eckhart, fourteenth-century mystic

Attention is the foundation of all the Qualities of Being. Pure attention is an attitude of focused receptivity and curiosity—an openness and availability to take in all that life offers without an agenda and without judgment. Attention, as a Quality of Being to utilize during times of darkness, is the behavior of observing and accurately labeling what we see and experience, without attempting to fix or change it. Small children are very good at giving this kind of attention to things that draw their interest. Children tend to approach the object of their interest with pure openness, having no previous experience upon which to base an evaluation. They are utterly curious and completely available to the moment at hand and the object of their interest. There is no holding back, and there are no preoccupations.

Bringing our awareness to something in this receptive, open manner is called beginner's mind. In Buddhism this term refers to the unusual success beginners often have when first coming to a spiritual practice. Beginner's mind is considered a blessing: long-term devotees of Buddhism endeavor to approach their spiritual routine as if they were beginners, letting go of past history with their spiritual practice as much as they can in order to experience it anew and keep it fresh and alive.

Pure attention is beneficial during times of crisis or challenge because it shifts our focus from self-absorbed anguish or worry about the future to what is actually around us. This shift creates a larger circle of life for us and makes us more receptive to Guidance. When we open up to all of life around us in this moment, it becomes easier to perceive the voice of the Divine Feminine and to recognize helpful Guidance as it appears in our lives.

Attention is powerful. In stage productions, using focused attention in this way is called giving focus. When the term is used in a dramatic context, it generally means that all actors onstage focus on the character toward which they want to draw audience attention. The simplest way in which this is done involves all the actors facing that character and listening, but it can also work if the actors all turn away from her. In the latter example, audience members will tend to look at the one person who stands out as different—the one being ignored.

In real life, giving our attention to something is usually an indication of interest or curiosity about that person or thing. When we are deeply focused on something we are interested in or curious about, we may lose track of time and even our usual self-consciousness, becoming fully absorbed in what we are doing or observing. Artists often speak about this experience of becoming one with the act of creating.

Attention given due to fascination or love is immediate and present. It is rooted in what is happening right now. By contrast, a person who is preoccupied seems to be completely unaware of the present moment around him, focused inwardly on something else. While it is possible to be focused inwardly on a present experience—as in meditation—usually such preoccupation indicates that a person has become engrossed in thoughts removed from the present, rehashing the past or planning the future.

When we experience darkness in our lives, it is common to become preoccupied with the past (how life was before the impact of these life challenges) or the future (what is going to happen now that life has been so completely changed). But while grieving a loss or struggling with change is essential to our growth, analyzing the past to see what one could have done differently and worrying about the future are fruitless tasks because we have no power over the past or the future. We do, however, have power in the present, and how we handle the present moment shapes our future experience. This moment's choice is the only one we have any influence over. *This* is the moment of power.

It is foreign to us as Westerners to focus on the present moment, and this is why it is so difficult for us to put our faith in and *do*. In Eastern traditions acceptance of one's circumstances and attention to the present moment are emphasized as valuable spiritual practices, but we are trained to plan for the future while keeping our past successes and failures in mind. In contrast, learning to focus our attention in the present moment simplifies our efforts and increases our peacefulness.

My own spiritual seeking has led me to understand that what I give my attention to always expands in my experience. I seem to get more of whatever I'm focusing upon. Could this be one reason that problems, both personally and on a global scale, seem to increase as we fight and resist them? The more we put our negative attention on what we don't want, the more of whatever we don't want there seems to be. Just as the character who is ignored in the stage play takes focus by being the different one, pointedly ignoring a problem — denial — gives focus and power to the problem. The attitude with which we approach problems seems to make a great deal of difference as to how these troublesome situations respond to the attention we give them.

By the time we're adults, most of us have learned to focus

on what *isn't* working in our lives in order to correct it, giving scant attention to what *is* working—what we enjoy, appreciate, and want to experience more. People don't understand why they keep getting more of what doesn't work, ignorant that their emotion-charged attention is a dynamic generator that causes what isn't working to increase. Even physics demonstrates that participatory observation does, indeed, influence the outcome of certain experiments. Physicist Fritjof Capra points out in his work *The Turning Point* that electrons spin on either a vertical or a horizontal axis, but it's impossible to determine the axis on which a particular electron is spinning by simply looking at it. The direction doesn't become apparent until a researcher begins to measure the spin. Whichever axis is chosen to measure, that's the one around which the spin appears. Was the electron always spinning around that axis? Or did the researcher's interactive attention unintentionally direct the spin? Since this happens virtually every time the experiment is performed, it appears to researchers that it is what they focus *their attention* upon that influences their result. Researchers are beginning to question how many other experiments may be influenced by the participatory observation of a supposedly objective researcher.

It is possible that our emotion-charged attention is a powerful influence in determining what experiences flourish and increase in our lives. If this is the case, we have an amazingly transformative tool at our disposal that can also influence the creation of what we find fulfilling and life enhancing. This is a worthwhile experiment to undertake. It is different from positive thinking, the act of repeating positive thoughts and ideas to ourselves, and while this is a good beginning, we usually have a lifetime of deeply held beliefs—both conscious and subconscious—containing a great deal of emotion, that contradict the positive thoughts we are repeating. Those old beliefs were developed over years, and a few weeks or months of erratic positive thinking won't be enough to permanently change our experiences.

Such change requires long-term practice. We must learn to substitute deeply felt new attitudes and beliefs for the old by repeating the new feelings and images that we want to experience more of in our lives. The task is to build *belief*. The words Jesus spoke to his disciples, "It is done unto you as you believe," and "When you pray, pray believing that you have the thing, and you will have it," also point us toward this idea: that to which you give your time, attention, and love (or any intense feeling—it can be positive or negative) increases in your experience.

When I was an acting student, I learned that one of the essential components of an effective performance is the actor's ability to take on a kind of temporary amnesia. Actors must approach their performances as if none of the conversations in the play have ever occurred before; as if none of the events taking place on the stage are known in advance to the actors. They must do this at *every* performance—sometimes eight performances a week for six months! This "acting as if" is a masterful act of directing one's own attention, which makes all the difference in creating a believable character. If actors don't convey that sense of immediacy to the audience, it will seem as if the characters are not real people. The play will feel flat and emotionless to those watching it.

This way of "acting as if" in daily life means knowing our own opinions and experience about a situation but simultaneously approaching that situation as if we know nothing about it, letting it be new and unpredictable. Making an attempt to see into circumstances without our historical references can allow us to perceive things we would otherwise have missed. We needn't succeed completely; the mere attempt to see our situation from another point of view can open us to new perceptions and information valuable to our success in moving more easily through the challenge. Our history with people, things, and circumstances becomes the filter through which we interpret them. This can cause us to miss things that someone who is new to the topic or relationship might see. Because of past experiences, we may also project meaning that isn't there onto an experience or situation, skewing our interpretation of what is actually happening. When we come to something freshly, we see it as it is in this moment, not bound to past history or future possibilities.

The Divine Feminine opens us to a realm of new possibilities and change. As we approach our challenges with the Guidance of the Divine Feminine, we may find that the future isn't always accurately predicted by looking at the past. Bringing our attention to the present moment without preconceived opinions and ideas is powerfully freeing. When we do this, our thinking is uncluttered. We observe what is before us more accurately.

Our past dictates a more rigid response to crisis. In our old model of behavior, when we found ourselves in the midst of a challenge, we might do one of two things. First, we might begin to struggle and plan, to suffer and exert effort, and to focus our attention on the outcome we desire instead of on the process in which we find ourselves. We focus on what worked in the past and on how to influence the future. Second, we might look ahead pessimistically to endless darkness, feeling there is no way out of our situation at all.

Instead of viewing the future with misery, or mounting a massive effort to control it by applying information from the past, we could choose to simply focus our attention on *this* moment, noticing what is happening and how it feels. End results are usually an experience of failure or triumph in a single moment, whereas the process of arriving at that end result is a series of now-moments. Attention, as a Quality of Being that helps us move through times of challenge, is behavior that, like meditation, requires us to keep noticing where our focus is—when we've wandered into the past or future—and bringing ourselves back to this moment. What can we do right now with the things that are happening today? When we begin to live in the present moment we are staying with the natural unfoldment, trusting the past and future to Spirit. It is in living the process this way, moment by moment, that satisfaction comes, and it is in allowing ourselves to be guided through our process that we gain the strength and wisdom needed for the next part of our journey, which is rarely known to us in advance.

As a culture, our typical approach to challenges is to generate an abundance of doing. We want to *do* and *do it now*, in a desperate effort to fix whatever we feel has gone wrong and has resulted in the challenge we are facing. But sometimes the correct action is to wait, to be still and watch. Watching and waiting can, however, be thwarted by a false urgency generated by the idea that we are the only one who can do it. This false idea can cause us to be reluctant to let go of our attempts to control the outcome. But we are constantly surrounded by the energy and possibilities of the entire Universe, and the Universe is capable of providing many people to help accomplish any task. We needn't work so hard all alone. We can allow ourselves to be guided by the Divine Feminine whose inclusiveness motivates us to work with others to develop solutions.

Openness to Guidance allows us to be attentive and ready to grasp that opportunity that is the solution to our current challenge when it arises. The solution can arise and present itself at any moment. But if we are actively resisting and manipulating our circumstances, trying to avoid repeating past mistakes, or reestablish past glory, or focus on anxiety about the future, trying to force a particular outcome, we may well overlook the solution when it comes. Being still and waiting for the right moment to take hold of an opportunity when it arises is the essence of good strategy and least effort.

Approaching attention as one of the tools for surviving tough times also introduces us to an uncommon experience of time that we may not have had since childhood. Chronos time, the logical and linear approach to time in which we measure our daily lives by clock and calendar, is our familiar experience in the Western world. Chronos time is divided into equal segments and allotted to particular activities. The clock and calendar set the everyday pulse of life, and every moment is seen as equal to every other.

However, in practicing attention to the present we may find ourselves experiencing kairos time. Kairos time is described by Stephen Covey in his book *First Things First* as "appropriate time." In the kairos model, time is experienced as a process. Its essence is how much value you get out of the time spent, rather than its essence being a measure of quantity. Kairos time is the familiar approach to time for most indigenous tribal peoples. It works by feel. We sense when the time is right to begin or end an activity. Kairos time is an organic way in which we can naturally respond to life.

In her book *Women's Reality* Ann Wilson Schaef says of kairos time, "Frequently the clock is irrelevant and may even be seen as interfering with the process of time. Early, late, and on time are concepts that have no meaning." Thus "How many hours did you work?" is a question whose answer would be measured in chronos time. "Did you have a good time?" can only be answered in the kairos time model.

Schaef makes the interesting point that the National Bureau of Standard's atomic clock — the most accurate time-measuring instrument in the world—still has to be set back a few seconds each year. So universal time is slowing down—it is not working in the chronos model.

Focusing attention on the now tends to generate the kairos experience of time, which is more peaceful and gentle to the self. In order to take on the tool of attention as an empowering Quality of Being, we must let go of the need to control the past and the future. This is the change in attitude that is required of us. If we cling to our need to control, we will be forever preoccupied by what has happened and what might happen. When we truly let go, the angel sentinel for this stage of our journey of healing gives us the Quality of Being tool that is attention. As we practice bringing our attention to the present moment, our perception begins to change, and so does our experience of life. We respond to the needs of this moment, minimizing influences from other times, people, and places that are not part of the current challenge. The new awareness we discover in changing our attitude and our behavior is a savoring and appreciation of the eternal *now*—the only time when we can receive Guidance. In the present we can never be short of time or out of it. It's never too late. And once we learn to live in the present, we can find our way back to it when we've strayed into the past or future.

Here are some simple ways to practice attention to the present moment:

1. Right now, breathe deeply and feel the movement of your body as you breathe. Close your eyes, and for one minute,

see how many different sounds you can hear. Which ones are near you and which ones are farther away?

2. If you are in a place where there are other people, take a moment to really look at them. Notice the colors and textures of their clothes. What do their facial expressions tell you about what they may be thinking or feeling?

3. Notice the temperature of the air around you. Notice where you can feel your clothing touching your body: your feet, your waist, your legs, shoulders, arms, wrists. Is your clothing soft or rough? Does it add warmth? Is it tight or loose fitting? If your hair is long, how does it feel against your neck, forehead, cheeks?

4. Put on some music and really listen to the way the instruments enter and retreat in turn. Listen to the words of the song. Focus and concentrate on the whole song. What is the music trying to communicate?

5. Sit down to a meal, and before eating, look at each of the foods on the plate. Notice the different colors and textures. Notice the different aromas, whether the food is warm or cold. Take a small bite and feel the food on your tongue — its texture and flavor. As you chew, savor the flavor of each bite.

6. Notice the different smells in the air. The ocean and the forest carry different aromas than does a city street, and different parts of the city may introduce different aromas, too. The restaurant district smells different from the train depot, the inside of a department store smells different in the fragrance department than it does where leather coats are sold.

See if you can identify any smells in the air around you right now.

7. When you are in conversation, look into the other person's face and listen to her words. Try to be attentive to *all* of the communication: gestures, tone of voice, word choices, facial expression, eye contact, and the content of the words. "Listen" to all of it.

8. When you are alone, "listen" to your own body. Where in your body are you loose, relaxed, and comfortable? Where are you tight and stiff? Do you feel refreshed or tired? Hungry or satisfied? Give attention to your emotional state. Do you feel interested in this day? Enthused about it? Are you preoccupied emotionally with a problem or relationship? Is the preoccupation pleasurable, painful, neutral?

The key to practicing attention is to come into this moment, right now, just as it is. When we notice that our attention has wandered away into fantasy, past history, or future hopefulness or dread, we simply bring it back to what is before us at this moment. Eventually this practice makes our attention obedient to our direction. We are then less at the mercy of our thoughts, which drag our attention and emotions after them, and have more choice about them, taking our attention away from critical, hurtful thoughts and memories, which increase bad feelings and behavior, and putting our attention on more life-affirming ideas that generate inspiration and gratitude. This is how practicing the Quality of Being of attention can bring healing back to us in a dark time.

There is usually a point in our darkness where we begin to crave the light and to seek it. Our attention can be irresistibly drawn to the light at the time when our vulnerability is the greatest. This combination of hunger and vulnerability is optimal for transformation. We are able and willing to consider things that in our usual daily way of living we might avoid or judge harshly. When we are off-balance and have lost control of things, the miraculous has room to move in us and in our lives. We are capable of receiving, loving, learning, and changing at a greater level than usual because we are focused, willing, and committed.

A wise teacher once said we should seek enlightenment with the kind of commitment a man would have who seeks water because his hair is on fire. Times of darkness can feel a lot like having one's hair on fire. We seek the light in such times, because we cannot stand to have things go on as they are. Often we realize that nothing we've done up till that moment has really changed our life positively the way we need something to change it now. *We* are what is needed to change our lives. Practicing attention during such a challenge is a potent way to take action and make progress toward resolution of that challenge.

Eight

Intention

....

Ultimately, human intentionality is the most powerful evolutionary force on this planet.

—*George Leonard,* The Life We Are Given

In its simplest definition, intention is the name for a clear, conscious commitment to a goal we wish to accomplish. Having intention means we plan to do whatever is needed, in alignment with our integrity, to bring about a particular result. When our intention to create a particular result in the world is clear, it organizes our priorities and our behavior in order to maximize the likelihood of that outcome. In the context of

Qualities of Being, intention includes the added complexity of nonattachment, or perhaps more realistically for our purpose of coming through a difficult time of darkness, low attachment. Nonattachment is a common tenet of Eastern faith traditions. It is the practice of actively letting go of trying to control something, while trusting that there is an inherent wisdom of God within us, within other people, and even within the situation in which we find ourselves, which inherently knows, naturally and organically, the best way to develop, heal, and resolve itself.

This is not the same thing as doing nothing and hoping for the best. On the contrary, the Quality of Intention requires that we work toward our identified goal while keeping our attention on the present moment. We must also work cooperatively with new developments while letting the final form of the outcome evolve naturally—even as we continue to work toward our revised personally envisioned form of that outcome. In doing this, we trust that the outcome, whatever it is, will be right exactly as it shows up, regardless of the final form.

The Serenity Prayer, used in many twelve-step programs, is one example of this committed involvement, coupled with the ability to let go and trust: "God grant me the serenity to accept the things I cannot change, the courage to change the things I can, and the wisdom to know the difference."

Let me give some other examples of how intention works and why it is powerful and liberating. Artists very often discover, in the course of creating a piece of art, that the creation begins to "do itself." The artist may begin with an idea of what he wants to create, but the creative process itself is nonlinear, which means that in the midst of the doing, the work may extend in a direction the artist hadn't foreseen at the outset of the project, yet it feels exactly right in the creative moment to flow in that new direction. The outcome is not what the artist first committed to, but by being flexible, attentive, and flowing with new developments in the creative process, the artist creates a work that may surpass his original idea.

Here's a second, very practical example. Over twelve years of ministry, every major event, celebration, or ceremony I've supervised happened in this way. We began with a purpose for the event in mind. We made specific plans. Each person or team involved in creating a part of that plan went off and did their very best. In every case, surprises occurred—some delightful, which added immensely to the beauty and effectiveness of our event, and some roadblocks, which caused us to think very creatively to solve the problems, revealing newness where we hadn't expected it. Even annual holiday events, which were the same in general format from year to year, manifested themselves in this way.

Anytime we begin work on something—and especially if that something is really important to us—we will find that this is how it goes. Rarely does the plan come off exactly as we have envisioned it. We will experience a great deal more peace in the creation process if we learn to anticipate and look forward to these "cosmic left turns" that force us to allow newness in and to be increasingly creative. These can become flashes of inspiration and genius.

In our personal times of darkness, it is particularly challenging to work with intention. We already feel vulnerable and shaky, and this aspect of the creative process asks us to be even more so. Yet perhaps because of our vulnerability our receptivity to the possible value of new ways of approaching our darkness may also be heightened. Healing is a creative process, and whether the healing we are experiencing is physical, emotional, spiritual, financial, mental, or social it works the same way. Healing is risk taking. It requires us to let go of what we know, and trust what we don't know. Intention is the clarity of mind and focus that allows us to consciously make the choice to work with our challenge in the framework of low attachment, while committing to a specific result.

The angel sentinel at the gateway to this passage in spiritual maturity requires that we give up the need for guaranteed outcomes, and the habit of quitting when things don't go our way. Instead, we are asked to embrace the wisdom of the Divine Feminine within us and within our situation to bring the right outcome for *everyone* concerned, whether we can see what that is or not. Remember that the Divine Feminine is holistic and inclusive. Allowing the influence of the Divine Feminine into our practice of intention means that no one in our lives who is also affected by the challenge we're experiencing will be left out of the healing process. To focus our efforts on our own healing while trying to ensure the punishment or hurt of another will not be effective in the realm of the Divine Feminine. Rather, it will backfire, causing us more trouble than we already have. To enter into the passageway of intention, we must trust the Guidance of the Divine Feminine to reveal to us the way to go, and then we must act upon that Guidance, intending that the result we come to will bless everyone concerned. Often this is a major shift in attitude.

When the angel sentinel gives us the gift of intention to practice as a consciously chosen behavior, we discover we must find a way to loosen our grip on the form of the outcome we want and get clearer about the feeling we want to experience in that outcome. Most of us attach our desires to a particular form of outcome because we believe that if we get our desire in just that form, we will feel happy, vindicated, satisfied, peaceful, content, safe—whatever way it is we want to feel but do not feel now. Unfortunately we never have full information about our own nature, let alone the nature of the universe, other people, the situation facing us, and their complex interrelationships, so it may be that the form we are attached to couldn't possibly bring us the experience for which we long. The Divine Feminine knows what will bring us that emotional experience, and in the most effective way. If we can remain involved in the process with a clear commitment to what we want to *experience* rather than how it has to *look*, we will be operating with intention.

High involvement/low attachment is one of four specific

ways of responding to a life challenge that I was introduced to by Michael Davis and Paulette Sun Davis, business and personal coaches with whom I have had the pleasure and honor of working. I choose to emphasize this particular way, which was taught as the most effective, because I have discovered its effectiveness in my own life. Michael and Paulette graphically teach their clients the ineffectiveness of reaching toward control as a goal by introducing a four-quadrant model of approaching challenges. The two axes of these quadrants are involvement and attachment (see Figure 1). The first quadrant in the upper left corner is the quadrant of low involvement and high attachment. This is the victim quadrant. Here we feel things must turn out the way we want them, but we don't participate in any way to bring that about. No authority, no responsibility, no involvement, but lots of attachment. In this place we behave manipulatively, believing we can't get what we want by being direct, and we have no power to influence the outcome except by getting others to do it for us. This is also the quadrant of complaint and blame.

The upper right corner is the quadrant of high involvement and high attachment. In this quadrant we participate fully in every way to force and push and influence the desired outcome. Here we are extremely attached to having that outcome show up exactly as we envision it. We constantly try to control the behavior of other people in order to ensure our outcome. The mental stress in this quadrant is unbelievable. This is the quadrant of the bully, or tyrant, and the quadrant of criticism.

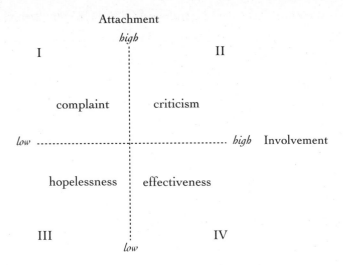

Figure 1. The horizontal axis measures level of involvement, from low to high left to right. The vertical axis measures level of attachment from low to high bottom to top. Quadrant I is low involvement/high attachment—the quadrant of complaint. Quadrant II is high involvement/high attachment—the quadrant of criticism. Quadrant III is low involvement/low attachment—the quadrant of hopelessness. Quadrant IV is high involvement/low attachment—the quadrant of effectiveness and fulfillment.

Quadrant three, in the lower left, is the quadrant of low involvement and low attachment. This is the home of apathy and indifference. The outcome doesn't matter to us, and we don't participate. In this quadrant we simply don't show up at all. We may comment and criticize, but we bring no energy, suggestions, or contribution to the conversation. We are deadweight. This is the quadrant of "So what?" and "Who cares?"

Here we may find people employed in jobs in which their opinions never influence anything that occurs. They have no authority and no real responsibility. They have learned over time the apparent futility of trying and have adapted to the pain caused by their lack of power by choosing not to engage, or care, at all. This is the quadrant of hopelessness, discouragement, and exhaustion.

The final quadrant, in the lower right, is the quadrant of high involvement and low attachment. Here, we participate fully with a goal in mind, but we let go of how the outcome manifests itself in form and we allow Spirit to guide its creation in the best way for all concerned. This is the quadrant of maximum fulfillment and effectiveness. We are focused on the present moment and fully engaged in it. We know what the goal is, but we leave the form of that result to God. Our job is to keep the intention clear while taking action fully in the present moment.

When we practice letting go of the need for a guaranteed outcome, and instead work toward the best outcome for all concerned and an experience of peace for ourselves, we find that our faith grows. Our responses to the demands of the moment become more balanced and we flow more gracefully with the unexpected. In such practice we find new awareness, a richer vision, and increased trust in God. The ups and downs of life ruffle us much less than they previously did. Not because we can control and predict what will happen but because we trust that whatever happens will be just right.

Commitment to an outcome always requires stepping away from the familiar into the new. The future is undefined, even while we try to ensure and define it. The risk of practicing intention is that things will turn out differently than we want them to, but perhaps they will turn out better than we could have imagined, too. Moving toward the future with intention means letting go of the status quo. The following stories are about two people who let go of the status quo and wandered into a new future. Each was committed to a new life, though neither knew how to get there. Each was backed into a corner because of darkness in his or her life.

The first story involves a letter to *Science of Mind Magazine*, telling how much benefit the writer had received from reading the magazine.

Dear Friend,

I found [this] beautiful magazine in a dirty run-down motel room. When I went into that room I was an alcoholic and an addict. When I left, I was a shining, clean and free woman. I was free from my obsession for alcohol and drugs. I was free for the first time in many years.

My life before this consisted of being locked up in hospital wards, jails and prisons several dozen times. One by one, I gave away my four children. During one of my more desperate times of loneliness I stole one of my children from her new mother. For this insanity I was sent to prison for child stealing.

I never knew what resentments were. What I felt was a deep hate for the whole world—but most of all for myself. I felt guilty, too, and knew what it was to be very lonely. The fears I had were many, and some were nameless. I made several attempts at suicide.

This was my life until I found that beautiful *Science of Mind Magazine* two years ago in that dirty little room. I read the words that told me God's dwelling place is within man, that if I would still my thoughts I would realize His Presence.

My friend, can you understand what those words meant to me when I had given up even the desire to live? Those words made me realize that God and I had never been separated. That we would never be apart in this world or any other world. I felt fear leave me; and a great stillness surrounded me. A river of peace flowed through me and streams of Light broke through the darkness and shone through me. I was healed. That Light has never left me, and each time I turn within to God's Presence I find the Light steady and undimmed by time. I know this Light is the Love that God has for man.

This Light has shone through to touch others and they are now healed as I have been. It is beautiful to see the images of God emerge from a form that is shaking and afraid and sick from ignorance. Sometimes I think I hear a mighty celestial cheer from the teachers of Truth from all ages as the miracle of God's Light shines through the darkness to heal another and still another.

May God bless you, my friend, and may He bless those wonderful people who wrote the words that started a chain of miracles.

With love,

Jane Doe

Jane's healing began when her life had hit rock bottom. But in order for healing to take place, Jane had to be ready to let go of the life she had been living—her status quo. Our status quo includes all the ways we usually try to control the world and other people around us. When Jane left that motel room, she couldn't have known what would happen next, but she was committed to the new idea that God's loving Presence was within her always, and couldn't be disrupted in any way. Living with that idea in mind changed her life. Her committed intention is what allowed the new to unfold. Without it, she would never have taken the action to stop drinking and using drugs.

The second story comes from Kevin, a congregant of mine who requested prayer before a serious surgery. These are the words he wrote not long after the surgery:

It was more than two months ago, before my surgery for cancer, that I submitted my first prayer request. Many wonderful things have taken place since then. . . . The surgery was a success and I am optimistic about a complete recovery after I go through some additional radiation therapy. During this challenging period, I have learned some things about prayer. I ask God to help me find the strength and courage *I already have* to help me through this period. When I look within myself for answers, hope, encouragement and other strengths already bestowed upon me by God, I seem to find instant peace and insight. This has been a great blessing.

Six months later Kevin wrote these words in an autobiographical essay,

People said, "It's too bad about Kevin." Even Kevin said that sometimes. His career hit a brick wall. His mood fell into a deep black hole. His energy seemed to flicker like a candle. But he kept looking for answers: alternative medicine, shark cartilage, Chinese herbs. He even went to church.

Well, maybe it was church, maybe not. Maybe it was one of those California ashrams because sometimes he came home humming strange chants. He even started meditating in quiet, empty rooms.

But after a while he said he felt better because he was praying for his health. He had a sudden burst of energy that he couldn't explain. Kevin told his doctor about a moment when he was just sitting on the couch and he suddenly felt his body fill with energy—like putting gas in a car—a wonderful moment that Kevin called instant healing. . . .

Kevin seems to be smiling more these days and is work-

ing again part-time. . . . We hear him laughing more often
and he doesn't seem to worry as much, especially about
what he calls the "little things" — like paying his bills, getting
stuck in traffic, and what other people think of him.

His color has come back and there's more *fire* in him
these days. . . . He is doing things he always postponed before — things like speaking up instead of holding back, taking time to travel on weekends, and just watching the
sunset at the beach.

Did he beat the cancer or didn't he? Nobody knows for
sure. Not yet. Funny thing, though. Lately we haven't
heard *anybody* say "It's too bad about Kevin." Not even
Kevin says that anymore.

Kevin didn't know what might work to improve his health,
but he was committed to finding and practicing it, whatever it
might be. Along the way some things worked and others
didn't, but Kevin kept going on the path to wholeness. Somewhere along the way the quality of his life began to improve.
Yes, he felt better physically, but it was more than that. He had
begun to live his life differently. His commitment to getting
well changed him. It revealed to him the many ways in which
he had not been taking care of himself. Although Kevin may
not be able to predict or control the end result of the cancer
treatments he has received, the life he is living is joyful and fulfilling. Clearly a healing has taken place.

The Divine Feminine directs the course of our healing
when we make the commitment and flow with what comes.

Staying with the intention requires courage when circumstances change our plans, but when we do so we are often led into richer territory than we knew existed. Courage—being filled with and led by the heart—is necessary to persisting with intention in the face of unpredictable occurrences.

Some simple ways of practicing courage and intention are:

1. Focus on what you want to *feel and experience* as your vision or desire manifests. Let go of what you think your vision should *look* like or *how it should come to you.*

2. Notice when "cosmic left turns" show up in a project, throwing a monkey wrench into your carefully laid plans. Ask "How can I make this change into a benefit?"

3. Breathe deeply when someone brings a conflict or problem into the plan. With two fingers, touch yourself an inch below your navel and apply gently pressure, bringing your attention to your center. Respond to the conflict only when you feel your attention has shifted to center.

4. Listen fully to objections and conflicts before speaking. Rather than being annoyed by a possible interruption to the progress of your vision, ask for clarification of any points you don't understand. Consider what is valid about the information. Ask yourself how this new information can improve the project.

Living with intention can be very difficult. In summary, to practice intention means to bring awareness repeatedly back to one's motivation and one's attachments, to honestly recognize our desire for control of the process of manifesting a vision as well as the form of that vision's outcome, and to purposely detach from the outcome while remaining involved in creating it. This practice might be too difficult to choose if the rewards of living with conscious intention were not so great. Experiencing more wonderful results than we alone could plan and control brings greater fulfillment into our lives.

Nine

Choice

....

I am the sum of my commitments, or in other words, I am
what I chose to stand up and be counted for, and those choices
define me.

—Martin Buber

The third Quality of Being is choice. Choosing is a conscious
action that distinguishes among options and commits to one or
more in order to move toward a desired outcome. Usually
choices are not made in a vacuum.

It is possible to fail to realize we have choices or to think in
very black-and-white terms and believe there are only two: the
right choice and the wrong choice. In order to know we have

a genuine choice, we must have the perception that our thoughts and feelings matter and that we have influence over what happens in our lives. Without this perception, we cannot exercise choice, even when it is right in front of us. When we know we have a choice, the very fact of knowing can change our perception of our circumstances, *even if we never make the choice to change those circumstances*. Likewise, perceiving that we have no choice influences our perception of our circumstances, even when that perception is incorrect.

In Tom Peter's and Robert Waterman's introduction to their book *In Search of Excellence*, they relate this example. "Adult subjects were given some complex puzzles to solve and a proofreading chore. In the background was a loud, randomly occurring distracting noise (two people speaking Spanish, one person speaking Armenian, a mimeograph machine, a desk calculator, a typewriter, and street noise). The subjects were split into two groups. Individuals in one set were just told to work at the task. Individuals in the other were provided with a button to push to turn off the noise. . . . The group with the off switch solved five times the number of puzzles as their cohorts and made but a tiny fraction of the number of proofreading errors." This is what one might expect if it weren't for what they go on to say. "None of the subjects in the off switch group ever used the switch. The mere knowledge that one (could) exert control made the difference."

None of the "off switch" subjects in the study tested the switch to see if their information and perceptions were correct.

They *believed* they had a choice that could influence their experience and that belief empowered them to perform better in the tasks at hand, even without actually exercising the choice to make a change in the situation. Those without the off switch *believed* they had no choices that would influence the environment in which they had to perform these tasks, and that belief handicapped them in performing the tasks effectively.

A second, more disturbing example of the power of our perception of the choices available to us comes from a congregant named Susan. Depressed by many failures in her attempts to overcome alcoholism, Susan decided to try living one day at a time. She finally succeeded in entering long-term recovery. By the time I knew her she was years into her recovery. Susan told me that what had allowed her to keep going was the knowledge that if she really couldn't take it anymore, she could always kill herself. She felt it was the one choice she knew she would always have, and knowing that she had that choice was comforting enough that she never had to act on it. This is a jarring example, but one with merit. I cannot tell how likely it was that Susan was really capable of acting on this choice, in fact I doubt if she knows that herself. But believing there was one choice left to her gave her the strength to try one more time, day by day.

The fact of having a choice is not necessarily the relevant factor; it is rather the *belief* in having that choice. So it stands to reason that perception of our ability to influence our experience via choice is an important factor in the process of successfully dealing with not only simple tasks but our experiences of genuine challenge as well. When we believe we can ease the difficulty of our experience through some choice or choices we may make, our perception of the difficulty we face may diminish.

But how do we cultivate awareness of the availability of meaningful choices? This stage of spiritual maturity, like attention and intention, is accomplished by entering a passageway of transition and practice. The angel sentinel at the gateway to this passage requires us to relinquish our attachment to our cherished identification as a victim. The Quality of Being we receive to work with is choice. Until we loosen our hold on the victim role, we cannot feel that our choices are meaningful and effective. Most of us have at least one area in our lives in which we blame other people for the results we've experienced. In other words, we feel we've been victimized by the behavior of other people. This may win us short-term sympathy or give us a reasonable excuse for our own limited thinking or behavior, but rather than helping us, this blaming subtly takes power away from us in the long run. It trains others to think of us as weakened. It trains us to think of ourselves as unable to adapt, heal, or grow beyond that point of victimization.

In the long run, we lose much more by holding on to our victim status than we gained from it originally. We may, in fact, have gained from it initially, because in many cases we *were* weakened at the time of the event in question. We needed the help and support of others to get through the event, and it was important that we had that help. But as time goes on after the victimizing event, the question becomes: when do we let go of the story of *what happened to us* as our identification of *who we are*? In order to progress, we must eventually realize that *we are more than what happened to us*. We are not defined by that experience. As long as we let the experience define us, it will weaken and disempower us.

It is scary to let go of our victim security blanket. What if we no longer identify ourselves to others as someone to whom *that* happened? Who are we without our wounds? How will we account for our strange quirks? Will we have to give up those quirks because we no longer have a good excuse for them? And how will we find our way to giving up those quirks? These are some of the challenging questions that choosing empowerment over victimhood can bring up.

On the other hand, to be set free from behaving and thinking of ourselves as victims is a transformative experience. Being free from victimhood means that what happened to us was real, but we are now moving beyond it, not only with lip service but in an effective, successful manner in our lives. This takes effort. It may require working with professionals dedicated to helping people through such experiences, rather than those who focus on the damage of the experience itself as "permanent."

I believe we are created by and out of a Divine Creative Presence. To me, this means that all the ideas and resources we need are already within us. The Divine Feminine is the presence of boundless possibilities. We live within the atmosphere of that Divine Feminine, but even more important, the Divine Feminine is within us. This means boundless possibilities exist right where we are at each moment. The most restricted human beings in prison or war-torn occupied countries still have the power of choice over what they think, feel, and believe. While it may be difficult to resist the pull of the crowd in such situations, it is still the choice of the individual what she will think. Survivors of concentration camps and prisoner-of-war camps have reported that what helped them survive and kept them sane were the things they chose to think about and put their attention on moment by moment, day by day.

It is with the Guidance of the Divine Feminine, that intuitive inner knowing, that we find what we need and use it effectively. The power to access and utilize this Guidance comes from our belief and perception that such Guidance is really there for us. Remember the "off switch" group? Their belief that they had power allowed them to respond more effectively to the challenge at hand. When we believe that the Divine Feminine is available to guide us, we are doubly blessed. First, the belief itself is empowering; second, we recognize and welcome the Guidance when it comes.

Making empowering choices means we take action, speak our minds, choose commitments, and honor ourselves actively in our lives, rather than wishing, hoping, blaming, and complaining about our lives. Living from choice redefines us. Empowerment and freedom become our new identification.

Practicing living from choice doesn't mean that we will never experience being victimized again. It can mean, however, that we now have the tools to move past such experiences and into healing and wholeness more quickly and with greater clarity. When we act from effective choices, letting go of ourselves as victim, we communicate honestly and fully seeking the win-win result for everyone concerned that I referred to in our discussion of intention. Working with others from a place of empowerment means we have the right to ask for what we want and the right to agree or say no to any request made by others. It also assumes others have the same rights. Living from choice gives us dignity and confidence in our ability to know what we want and to choose it wisely and responsibly.

Some practices for increasing our awareness of choice are based upon changing habitual patterns:

- Choose to drive to work by a new route.
- Go to a favorite restaurant and order something from the menu that you've never eaten before.
- Take a trip to a place other than your typical vacation spots.
- Change your work schedule. Instead of coming in at 8:00 and leaving at 5:00, come in at 10:00 and leave at 7:00.
- Say yes to a friend's invitation to go somewhere or do something you don't normally think of as "you."
- Go to see a movie that's not typically your style.

- Ask directly for what you want in a situation where you'd usually keep quiet and hope or dread.
- Express your opinion about current events or entertainments even when they are different from the prevailing opinion in your circle of friends.
- If you typically buy clothing or household items in every style and color so as not to have to choose, choose your favorite and buy only that one.
- If you typically buy the cheapest item rather than assessing colors and styles, commit to buying your favorite color instead.
- Seek workshops and counseling that help you unravel your attachment to past experiences in which you felt victimized.

The effectiveness of believing that you have a choice comes with making unfamiliar choices in areas in which you customarily feel the decisions are already made. You know what you usually do in those circumstances, and you usually continue to do those familiar things. But practicing making different small choices and stretching yourself a little will allow you to develop the skill and courage to make new choices in more challenging situations.

This practice may at first feel uncomfortable, but as you continue to do it you can begin to experience freedom and progress. Feelings of stale stuckness can be traded in for a discovery of possibilities in yourself you didn't realize were there.

Becoming empowered after having once given up our power and claimed the victim label can feel strange and awkward, like learning anything new. But restoring a feeling of effectiveness and control in our lives is worth the discomfort required to achieve it.

A therapist friend of mine was telling me recently about new research that indicates that a traumatic event in one's life triggers a certain reasonable level of automatic protective response from the body-mind, but if traumatic events occur repeatedly, soon only half the provocation is necessary to bring about twice the response. Eventually with multiple repeated stressors, the slightest trigger can provoke a person into an immense reaction—one entirely out of proportion to the triggering event in that one situation. In order to unplug from this accelerating cycle, individuals need to find ways to communicate about traumatic events, not just once but over and over again. As they do so, they begin to unplug themselves from the reactiveness that was triggered by the event itself, and return to their more centered selves. This is why grieving people need to talk over and over about who or what it is they have lost. It is our inborn inclination to do this in order to heal ourselves. To talk about such things rather than trying to swallow our feelings about them is a choice. It requires effort to maintain that choice and act on it.

When we are in crisis, we may not feel we know what we want, or how to make important decisions. This is the time to continue to talk about what we are *feeling and experiencing*—

even if what we are feeling and experiencing is numbness and confusion. Doing so will help remove the blocks to making choices, as well as to help us move through the trauma we are experiencing without building up a residue of sensitivity and pain. We must have the help and support of others to carry out our choices successfully, and we must take into consideration the effect the choices we make have upon others, as well as upon our own lives. Look for family members, friends, counselors, therapists, spiritual leaders, chaplains, and others who are able to listen during times of challenge, especially those who can listen without hurrying you out of your feelings. This experience alone will do much to renew your faith in your ability to cope and make good decisions.

Practice making choices whenever they are offered to you, no matter how simple. Suggest additional choices when what is presented to you seems limited or unacceptable. Choose experiences outside your familiar routine. Eventually the discomfort of the unfamiliar will diminish as your belief in choice as a part of who you are begins to grow.

Ten

Practice

....

For one who is on the master's journey . . . the word [practice]
is best conceived of as a noun, not as something you *do*, but as
something you *have*, as something you *are*. In this sense, the
word is akin to the Chinese word *tao*, and the Japanese word
do, both of which mean, literally, road or path. Practice is the
path upon which you travel, just that.

—*George Leonard*, The Life We Are Given

The act of practice is a lifelong commitment to honor and
grow into a way of living. It is the formation of a positive habit
that becomes a personal tradition of deepening, discovery, and
perhaps ultimately, mastery. Throughout this book, I have
stressed the importance of practice to the success of each
Quality of Being and each transformative way of thinking and
acting. Practice itself is also one of the Qualities of Being.
While it is true that some of us may come upon a skill naturally

and don't need to practice much to be good at it, this is rare. Most of us need to consciously practice new skills in order for them to become second nature. This is particularly true when the skills expand us spiritually, because spiritual improvement isn't always as readily observable as with a physical skill.

At first we may be awkward and inconsistent at applying our budding abilities. Remember learning to drive a car? At the beginning you probably had to consciously concentrate on steering, braking, observing the speed limit, checking mirrors, signaling—and all of it seemed like a lot to be aware of simultaneously. If you learned to drive on a standard transmission, the process was even more complicated, as both hands and feet had different jobs to do. Over time, though, it got easier. These days you probably drive to and from work and various errands on a daily basis without giving much thought to the processes of braking and turning, not to mention operating a radio, heater, and maybe even talking on the phone at the same time.

With the Qualities of Being, we are developing new skills for responding to the upheaval of difficult challenges. Like the freedom we felt as teenagers learning to drive—with all the enticing promise of being able to go wherever we wanted—the Qualities of Being provide us with increased freedom, enabling us to respond to the unpredictable changes in life with more flexibility and peacefulness, and thereby helping us go on with our lives in the way we most want to, from choice rather than out of a feeling of fate or doom.

Practice is one of the keys that allows this magic to take

place. As Michael Murphy says in *The Life We Are Given,* "Practice is a seedbed of miracles." The amazing way in which the human brain is designed allows us to literally internalize what we've learned and remember it effortlessly for future reference. This information has been confirmed for me by numerous medical professionals. Here's how it works. Nerve connections grow and develop in the brain as a result of stimulation. The more varied and abundant the stimulation, the more nerve connections are created, the more choices and abilities we develop. When a baby makes a verbal sound and gets a positive response from the adults around him, he is likely to repeat that sound. As he does so, there is a physical response in his brain to this repetition.

As the action is repeated, the human brain is triggered by the repeated firing of the same sequence of neurons within it that are required to accomplish making that sound. The baby continues experimenting with the sound, and the repeated firing of the same neuron sequence eventually wears an actual groove in the brain, making it increasingly easy for the baby to repeat that sound as the neuron sequence firing becomes faster and more automatic. This process is the same whether the repeated action is making a single sound or learning to speak, walk, or dance. The repeated firing of sequential neurons, over time, creates a "pathway" in the brain. And like a favorite pathway through a field, the more a sequence of neurons is used, the more worn and easy to traverse that groove in the brain becomes.

This empowers us to learn and to form habits. Repetition also increases the ease with which we can do the activity the next time because repetition deepens the groove in the brain and increases the speed at which the neurons along that pathway can respond and fire. Since there is less and less physical resistance to the sequence of neurons firing, the neurons begin to respond with lightning speed and accuracy as soon as the beginning of the familiar activity occurs. Once a habit is formed there is no need to think about it in order to do it. This is why we no longer have to concentrate so hard when we're driving in order to do it well.

If we were choosing to create a new pathway through a field, the going would be difficult. We might need to hack our way in with a machete to get through all the grasses and brush, and it could be a lot of work. With persistence, we would, indeed, have a new path, but if we happened to give up, the work we had done would deteriorate, and the field would quickly return to its original state. Should we persist with the path, the further we got with the work the easier it would become. Once finished, however, we would have to use the path with regularity to keep it open and free flowing.

This analogy describes what literally happens in the brain as we learn and practice new skills. Similarly the old abandoned sequential neuron groove of a discarded habit, when no longer used, will eventually become overgrown, and therefore less easy to use than in the past, much like an abandoned overgrown path in a field or in the woods. Because this is true, it is possible for us to break old habits permanently. Making the change is difficult initially, because the brain is conditioned to quickly respond to the old stimulus. But as we practice refraining from the old habit, the brain eventually stops reacting so quickly in anticipation of the familiar sequence. The longer we leave that specific neuron sequence unused, the easier it will become to do so. The new behavior with which we replace the old habit then forms its own groove in the brain as it is repeated, supporting the new choice of action and making it easier to repeat each time in the future. This is one aspect of how we change.

What is true of the brain for physical activities like playing a musical instrument, learning a sport, or becoming proficient at math, is true for thought as well. A repeated thought also creates a physical groove in the brain, making it easier to think that thought in the future. Beliefs, like physical habits, are developed through repetition. As children, we hear ideas and beliefs put forth by family members, teachers, and friends. Some of these ideas we think over repeatedly on our own, particularly those to which we have a positive or negative emotional reaction. These repetitions trigger the brain's physical support system for us to retain and repeat those thoughts, creating neuron connections in rapid sequence. Beliefs created by repetition and established physically in the brain become our reality. They seem like the Truth to us, so familiar and easy do they become over time. The downside of this miracle is that our brains are designed to support our choices of thought and action no matter what they are, simply responding to the process of repetition itself. So it is possible for us to establish beliefs that are inaccurate and even harmful to ourselves, and to have difficulty ridding ourselves of them, even when we discover as adults that they are false or damaging.

This is why practice is so important to establishing new ways of responding in thought, attitude, and action when challenges come. Without practice, most of us will revert to our usual response pattern when under stress. If this response pattern is unproductive, we can find ourselves in increased pain and despair as our old habits reinforce the unhealthy pattern. Practice of a new skill, or skills, gives us another possibility and opportunity. Because the old habit becomes less familiar over time, we begin to respond—at first like a new driver, consciously and carefully—choosing the alternative skill we wish to establish.

In the beginning, sometimes we will be successful with the new skill, and sometimes we will revert back to our old habit. This part of the learning process can be maddening. We see clearly the choice we wish to make, but we discover ourselves doing exactly what we want to release and avoid. Be patient with yourself when this happens. The very fact that it frustrates you is evidence that you are making progress. There was a time, before you began to make the change, when you were unaware that such a change would truly be more valuable to you than the old habit. Now that you are aware, you are creating that new internal pathway. Even with your intention to establish the new behavior clearly in mind, sometimes the old response will feel so easy and familiar that you will take it out of habit.

Practice, by its very nature, takes time. Practice, by its very nature, yields results—but not smoothly, and not all at once. This idea is well expressed by Portia Nelson in her poem "Autobiography in Five Short Chapters":

Chapter 1

I walk down the street.
There is a deep hole in the sidewalk.
I fall in.
I am lost . . . I am helpless.
It isn't my fault.
But it takes forever to find a way out.

Chapter 2

I walk down the same street.
There is a deep hole in the sidewalk.
I pretend I don't see it.
I fall in, again.
I can't believe I am in this same place.
It isn't my fault.
But it still takes a long time to get out.

Chapter 3

I walk down the same street.
There is a deep hole in the sidewalk.
I see it is there.
I fall in . . . it's a habit . . . but now my eyes are open.
I know where I am.
It is my fault.
I get out immediately.

Chapter 4

I walk down the same street.
There is a deep hole in the sidewalk.
I walk around it.

Chapter 5

I walk down a different street.

It is through the process of conscious repetition that we become aware of the possibility of different choices and we begin to make them. In fact, as we continue our practice, choices we never knew existed can become visible to us for the first time. The process is challenging, since growing into transformation is always more difficult than simply repeating the past.

In George Leonard's and Michael Murphy's book, *The Life*

We Are Given, Leonard states, "Your resistance to change is likely to reach its peak when significant change is imminent." This idea is one I find inspirational in its ability to motivate me to continue through the more difficult parts of creating a new behavior or thought pattern. In Leonard's earlier work, *Mastery,* he outlines the pattern of improvement yielded by consistent practice as one in which progress is followed by long periods of plateau, then followed by an unpredictable and sudden leap in improvement. We don't completely maintain the new level after that leap, however. We soon settle in at a level higher than the previous plateau, but not quite as high as the progress we experienced in the moment of the leap. We have glimpsed the future, but we cannot keep it yet. Now we find ourselves on a new plateau, and we may stay there for a long time before the next leap.

While this isn't the constant upward progress most of us hope to make when we initiate a change in thinking or behavior, it is realistic in terms of the usual flow and pauses we experience in the process of practice. When we realize this and expect it, we can more easily enjoy the practice itself, and, remembering that living from intention means letting go of controlling the outcome, we can allow the natural course of practice to bring the outcome to us in a timely way, while remaining in the present with the experience of practice itself.

"Where does the Divine Feminine fit into practice?" you may be asking yourself. The Divine Feminine is inherent in process and practice. It follows the Quality of Being of attention and becomes the heart of entering the now moment and savoring it, whatever may be going on, full of faith that the next moment is already taken care of as it grows organically out of this one. When we engage in practice, we are immersing ourselves in the Divine Feminine approach to life. In order to do so, our "I want it now" thinking must fade into the background. The urgency to be at the end of the process instead of experiencing it one moment at a time must be traded in for giving full attention to the practice itself. The cyclical rhythm of practice becomes satisfying and soothing. As we commit to our practice with the full intention of improvement and full commitment to stick with it, results come in their own time, but they come. We create a foundation of knowledge and stability. We can respond quickly with less effort in ways we've consciously chosen, rather than from reaction. We find ourselves living the life we've actively committed to participating in via our practice.

Practice is the committed, consistent repetition of the new choice we wish to establish over a long period of time, perhaps for the rest of our life. When we are looking for an action to take in the midst of darkness, spiritual practices such as meditation, yoga, prayer, affirmations, and visualization will help. Sometimes the practice is simply that of enduring with faith and surrender. To sustain practice, the practice itself must become the goal and the pleasure, not the outcome for which we strive. This is true because when the end result is the only motivation for practice and progress is slow, we are always tempted to give up the practice. In contrast, if the practice itself is our goal, our attention becomes focused on the present moment rather than the future. Our goal is accomplished merely by giving ourselves over to the practice, no matter how well or poorly a particular practice goes.

At the gate of the Quality of Being of practice, the angel sentinel informs us that we must leave behind our craving for instant results. As we enter into regular practice, we discover we are learning to savor the process of unfoldment, to treasure the process of our own transformation. As we continue living in practice, we discover that its eventual reward is mastery. Mastery is not a finite end point but a dynamic, living place of awareness and behavior that begins to shape our choices in every area of life, not just the one area we set out to change. To quote George Leonard again, "Mastery isn't reserved for the supertalented. It's available to anyone who is willing to get on the path and stay on it—regardless of age, sex, or previous experience."

These are some of the things you can do to begin to enter into practice as part of your daily life:

- practice not rushing—no hurry—attend to what you're doing as you prepare to go to the next activity
- meditate daily
- begin a sport or workout routine that requires participation at least twice a week
- take a class in something you've always wanted to learn,

like a new language, art form, or ethnic cooking class, and
make time to use what you learn in your everyday life

- take an art, dance, drama, music, photography, or other
  creative class and do some of it every week for the purpose
  of full participation and enjoyment regardless of how well
  or poorly you do it

Centering yourself spiritually becomes a rejuvenating
process in the midst of times of challenge. Practicing in this
way before challenges begin allows us to live our lives responding in a chosen manner to life's ups and downs. When
we have been doing this and a crisis occurs, the crisis will still
shake us, but our practice will give us the comfort of the familiar and consistent while providing us with the strength and
increased clarity we need to make good decisions.

If you have not yet begun a practice and a crisis arises, you
can immediately develop a simple minipractice to use automatically, whether the challenge is an upset at the office, a
quarrel with a friend, or a deeper trauma like serious illness
in the family. For initiating immediate practice, try the following:

- stand and stretch every thirty minutes during your work-
  day throughout the time of the crisis, whether for that day
  only or for a number of months
- breathe deeply
- drink more water than you usually do

- notice when you begin to worry and choose instead to turn your mind to a comforting thought
- notice when you begin to feel hungry, cold, or tired, and immediately do something to meet that need lovingly

Remember that to be a practice the activity must be repeated often, so let yourself continue these behaviors throughout the time of crisis, whatever its length. You may find you want to continue them even beyond the duration of the challenge because they are nurturing, self-compassionate practices. The Divine Feminine loves this nonlinear, process-oriented way of approaching the "doing" in our lives, because it is the natural way of living in the present moment and treasuring what each moment happens to bring. Such a practice allows us to respond as clearly and cleanly as we wish to the actual challenge at hand, instead of automatically reacting as if to a similar past experience, or something we fear may happen that hasn't happened at all.

As we persist with the full intention of improvement, we lean into those plateaus in our practice rather than pulling away and resisting them. We learn to deepen ourselves there. We become familiar with all the nuances of our practice at that level. Then, suddenly, we break through into a new level of ability and skill.

Eleven

Surrender

....

Be patient with all that is unresolved in your heart
And try to love the questions themselves
Do not seek for the answers that cannot be given
For you would not be able to live them
And the point is to live everything
Live the questions now
And perhaps without knowing it
You will live along some day
Into the answers.

—*Ranier Maria Rilke, "Letters on Love"*

Perhaps one of the most important and challenging of the Qualities of Being is surrender. I have used a variety of words throughout these pages to refer to surrender, including letting go and releasing. Each of these words refers to the action of giving up the illusion of, and the effort to, control. We grab in order to control something when we feel afraid that we are about to lose our influence over it. To prevent that loss, we attempt to assert or maintain control over a person, idea, situation, or project. Controlling is usually counterproductive and seldom truly effective. It may bring a temporary (false) sense of security, but it cannot bring the genuine sense of peace of mind and safety we're seeking when we make the grab for control. Surrender is a part of every one of the other Qualities of Being, but it stands on its own as well.

A common fear that arises when people think of surrender is that it means to quit—to lie down and die. This is not the surrender to which I refer. In my faith tradition we have two sayings that seem to contradict each other. The first is "Let go and let God," and the second is "Treat [pray] and move your feet." I often explain the harmony between these ideas by saying that in order to receive the Guidance we need to make wise decisions, we must pray and listen. We must become receptive. We must let go of our own ideas of how things have to be in order to be able to hear a higher voice, let that divine voice in. This is the "let go and let God" part of the work. Then we must take action on the Guidance we've received. We must "move our feet" once the prayer is done and the Guidance sought. After the action is taken, we must, once again, let go and let God do the work that comes after our action. A balance in mature spiritual practice calls for both the ability to let go completely of our own attachments to what we want, and the ability to act on inner Guidance once we've received it. This letting go is the surrender of which I speak.

One of my favorite joyful images of surrender comes from

Disneyland. There is a huge indoor roller coaster at Disney-land called Space Mountain that you ride entirely in the dark. Around you on the curved walls and ceiling are projections of the night sky: stars and galaxies swirl past as you spin on-ward without knowing what is coming next. Although I am usually something of a control freak in my own life, I like to sit in the front of the first car on this ride, so I can't possibly tell what's coming next. The ride spins in increasingly faster circles one way and another. I know I have no control over what happens next, but securely belted in I feel safe, so I aban-don myself totally to the experience, shrieking with the sur-prises and exhilaration.

I feel less safe in everyday life to simply let go and thor-oughly enjoy wherever the ride takes me, but this, I think, is the ultimate surrender in life: realizing we are spiritual beings in human form and experience for a short time, and entering into any experience fully and without resistance. I look for-ward to the day when I can live my life with less caution about what might happen and more curiosity about what's next. Practicing surrender on a daily basis helps me grow in my ability to do that.

In the realm of the Divine Feminine the joy of surrender contains no fear of hurt, destruction, loss, or betrayal. The Divine Feminine is not separate from anything that exists. Consequently, in the Divine Feminine there is nothing to fear or resist—nothing that can ultimately harm or damage that boundless Presence that is the essence of who we are as well.

The Divine Feminine flows utterly without resistance to whatever arises. Since we are enfolded in that Presence, and it flows through us, as us, we can surrender into it in perfect safety. There we can open to the Guidance we need. We might look at surrender this way:

Surrender is being at one with what is happening rather than pulling away from it.
Surrender is entering fully into the experience with complete abandon.
Surrender is entering into a realm beyond winning and losing where there is only One.
Surrender is waiting on Spirit.
Surrender is opening to synergy.
Surrender is allowing for the possibility of miracles.
Surrender is letting it happen, rather than making it happen.
Surrender is discovering what's possible.
Surrender is discovering what you can do.
Surrender is letting go of reasons and excuses.
Surrender is having nothing to lose and being fearless.
Surrender is peace.
Surrender is opening to the truth.
Surrender is the possibility of more.

Letting go into the Divine Feminine and surrendering to the Guidance that is available for us there, rather than trying to figure things out and manipulate them, may feel frightening because we have been taught that negative, painful occurrences in our lives are God's will. This explanation for suffering in the world often does little to ease the burden of our pain or satisfactorily answer our perennial questions, "Why does suffering exist? Why is this happening to me?" I have heard some plausible theories as to why negative things occur, but I have yet to hear a genuinely complete and satisfactory explanation for our pain. More helpful questions might therefore be, "How can our suffering be eased or relieved?" or "How can I change my viewpoint about what is happening to me in order to open up more positive choices?"

Dr. Peggy Bassett, a ministerial mentor of mine, used to say, "Pain is inevitable. Suffering is optional." While this phrase may sound glib, it has merit when we look into it. The difference between pain and suffering is in the mind — the thoughts and interpretations — of the one experiencing the pain. How we come to the pain we experience makes all the difference as to whether that pain becomes suffering or not.

What we must let go of, then, at the gate of surrender in order to enter into the passageway of this step in spiritual maturing, is the need to be right. This letting go is an ongoing practice, as it is for each attitude we've released at each gate we've passed through on the journey to wholeness. When we are no longer dominated by the need to be right, endless possibilities stretch out before us. Surrender is letting go the need to understand and be understood; the need to figure things out and to explain them; the need to bolster up our own explanations for things.

Here's why the quest to explain things and people can sometimes become a roadblock to resolution and reconciliation. When we don't understand something, we may use that lack of understanding as a roadblock to action that needs to be taken. We may hold back until something makes sense to us before we respond. But some things and people we simply are not going to understand. Sometimes people are not going to understand us, no matter what we do to try to help them get it. We have vast differences with some of the people with whom we share this planet. We may never see eye to eye, or share the same worldview. But a lack of understanding need not equate to a lack of cooperation or compassion, nor need it reduce our desire to listen and make space for another person's way of seeing something.

When we insist on understanding as a prerequisite to acceptance of another person or the situation in which we find ourselves, we may postpone or prevent our ability to respond with compassion, tolerance, gratitude, and trust. The practice of surrender develops in us a flexibility within which there is unlimited freedom and possibility. Living in surrender opens the door to experiences we haven't imagined because we can't yet understand them. There is much that exists beyond the realm of our understanding. Would we deny ourselves all experience of such miracles because we don't know how they occur?

Another of my colleagues, Dr. Jesse Jennings, told a story of a friend of his who had made the decision to believe in angels, "not because any angels had appeared to him to furnish proof of their existence," Jesse said, "but because he decided that even if they did exist, he'd never see one as long as he believed they didn't." That's one way of surrendering to a possibility in order to keep your options open!

Surrender not only moves us beyond the need to understand, it allows us to realize we can't control something by explaining it. For too many years human personal prejudices have been justified by what we thought were good explanations. We've justified such prejudices with everything from the U.S. Constitution to the Bible. But our hearts somehow know that these justifications, logical though we may believe them to be, are simply wrong when such authoritative documents are used to disenfranchise and control others by explaining away our mistreatment of people. We've made room for ourselves to judge and attempt to control others based on our "understanding"—our "rightness." When we surrender to the truth that we don't completely understand, and are unable to ensure the rightness of our opinions, we stand on the threshold of discovery. From here we can begin to see others and ourselves more clearly.

Surrender is freeing. It reflects deep trust in the Infinite, which increases the feelings of safety we tried to create by being right. It opens us to hear our genuine Guidance and to be receptive to the revealing of Truths we've yet to encounter.

In the November 1995 issue of *Guideposts* magazine, an article appeared that deeply touched me. It was called "Someone Hates Us!" The article told of a man so consumed by hatred that he made anonymous, harassing phone calls and sent hate mail to neighbors who were Jewish and Vietnamese and to a local prominent black woman. He made a name for himself in his community by sponsoring a white supremacist video series on the local public access station.

The man was Larry Trapp, a Grand Dragon of the Ku Klux Klan. Severely diabetic, legless, and going blind, Larry was considered extremely dangerous by law enforcement authorities. He kept an arsenal of loaded guns and Nazi paraphernalia in his apartment.

The woman writing about him was Julie Michael-Weisser, the mother of a Jewish family who had moved into town. Julie, her husband, Michael, and their three children knew they were being threatened, yet their curiosity about what could make a human being so hateful got the better of them. Michael began to call Larry and leave thought-provoking messages on his answering machine. "You know, Larry," Michael would say, "with your disabilities, the Nazis would have made you the first to go," and "Why do you hate me? You don't even know me." He kept up these calls for months until one day Larry answered the phone and accused Michael of harassment. At Julie's suggestion, Michael replied, "I don't want to harass you. I was thinking you might need a hand with something. Can I take you to the grocery store?" After a silence, Larry's voice changed slightly. "I've got that taken care of, but thanks for asking. . . ."

Not long after the initial phone call, Larry took his white supremacist video program off the air. Michael called to offer his support of Larry's change of heart and was rebuffed, but he heard something in Larry's voice that made him think Larry was softening. These events led to several other conversations, which shifted something in the Weisser family. Originally they had begun contacting Larry in hurt and anger, but now they were beginning to care about him. One evening at their synagogue, Michael was moved to request prayer for Larry from his congregation. "Pray tonight for someone who is sick from the illness of bigotry and hatred. Please pray that he can be healed." The next night, Larry called asking to speak with Michael. He would allow the Weissers to visit him.

That visit was the beginning of massive changes in all their lives. Larry broke into tears and apologized for all he had done. Over the next months he took down his KKK and Nazi paraphernalia and apologized to everyone he had harmed. Larry became a part of the Weisser family. He went to services at the synagogue with them, studied Judaism, and, as his health deteriorated, moved in with the family so they could help care for him. Doctors estimated Larry had only a few months to live, so Julie took time off from work to be with him, hearing the horror stories of Larry's childhood and, over time, coming to forgive him. More important, she says, Larry forgave himself. While he was still mobile enough to go out on his own, he returned from an outing with a bouquet of yellow roses for Julie and a note that read, "To the most beautiful woman, who helped me in my transformation from a dragon to a butterfly." The morning Larry died, Michael was at his bedside, holding his hand.

When I shared this story with my congregation, it moved them. Even my son, as a young teenager, was riveted by the story of a transformed life—one that began in hatred and ended in love. For me, the story is an example of how surrendering our need to be right can allow us to reach out in compassion and discover larger truths than we could see from our place of "rightness." Both Larry and the Weisser family felt "right," and both had reasons for their opinions. It wasn't until they each began to make space for the person they disliked or didn't understand that miracles could happen. From the place of being rooted in "rightness" all of them could easily have continued to stand in opposition to one another, assuming they understood what the other was all about. From the place of surrender, though, the Divine Feminine could guide their hearts to a new place of discovering, reconciliation, and awareness. Healing occurred in Larry Trapp, and it was a divine transformation, but healing also occurred in the Weisser family as they allowed the Infinite, through their inner Guidance, to show them how to respond to Larry in ways that could reach through the armor surrounding his heart. It was their surrender to Guidance that allowed this to take place

Surrender is the ability to let go and allow something larger than ourselves to guide us when what we've been doing isn't working. It means knowing there may be a better way than anything we can think of, and it means that the way through a challenging situation may sometimes appear to be walking right into the center of the fire.

Most of us want to have complete control over our lives, yet this control is an illusion. As we have seen, the way of the Divine Feminine is letting go into the moment completely with abandon and trust, knowing that all is always ultimately well.

Surrender in times of crisis opens us up to the Guidance we need to make good choices. The Guidance that comes to us in times of surrender responds specifically to our personal need; for the Weissers, ideas about how to respond to Larry simply came to them. The Infinite knows how to bring us clues to our Guidance that are gentle but are also tailored to our personal way of seeing and knowing so that we won't miss them. We can recognize these clues and feel their rightness even when we don't understand everything about them.

When we practice surrender day to day, we begin to build a skill for turning things over to the Infinite and listening for direction. This provides us with the strength we need to do the same in times of crisis. But even if we haven't practiced surrender before a challenging time enters our lives, we can begin to access this tool when the crisis comes. Surrender means realizing that although we may not know the answer to our personal challenge, the Infinite knows. When we say that the Infinite is omnipresent, it means that the Divine One is right where we are and It knows the answer we need. We let go, knowing that the Divine One is within us as well as around us, so the answer to our challenge is also known within us. We wait and watch and make the best decisions we can, trusting that the Infinite is bringing us the resources, ideas, and wisdom to make those decisions successfully. This type of letting go into the Divine paradoxically brings an increasing sense of safety. Some of the ways we can practice surrender are:

- When you disagree strongly with someone, instead of arguing, say, "Tell me more about how you see that," opening to how the other viewpoint was formed.

- When something doesn't go as planned, *breathe*, and consider the possibility that what is happening is an opportunity for a better result. Ask yourself the following questions: How could you open up to the possibilities being presented? How could you seize the opportunity, rather than remaining stuck on what isn't working?

- When a person's behavior evokes your disapproval, ask yourself, "How does this person's behavior empower her in her own eyes? How does it forward her life? How might she see this behavior as forwarding her own life for greater good?"

- When someone expresses strong disagreement with or disapproval of you, *breathe*. Rather than defending yourself, ask yourself, "How might my opinion or behavior be seen by this person as an attack on him or on his values?"

My mother used to say that little children are "bound and determined to have their own way about things." She also used to say that older people are "set in their ways." These phrases seem to me to be saying the same things. And for the people in the years between childhood and old age, wanting things to go our way all the time is simply seen as stubborn selfishness. Yet the desire goes on. We want what we want how we want it and when we want it. When we don't get it, we are likely to have a tantrum of some sort, no matter what our age. But the real gold is in the moments after the tantrum. After the frustration erupts, what then? That is the moment to recognize what is happening, and choose surrender. That is the moment when Guidance and the healing power of transformative miracles can occur. That is when we can realize that although we may not understand, we can still respond effectively to any crisis and see a positive outcome.

Twelve

Intuition

....

If you build it, he will come.
—Field of Dreams, *film*

Women's intuition" was a phrase used until it became politically incorrect to attribute illogical and sometimes supersti-
tious thinking to the female gender. Today intuition has lost its
gender specificity and gained an increased measure of respect,
or at least tolerance. Leaders in a variety of fields have acknowledged they often come to their most influential and life-
impacting decisions, discoveries, and investments based on

strong feelings, hunches, dreams, gut instinct, and that non-linear knowing that is so difficult to explain to someone who wants to know *how* you arrived at your conclusion. Intuition is the spontaneous appearance of knowledge: a new idea, the solution to a problem, a clear sense of where to go or what to do next, in the absence of sufficient background or information to *think* one's way to that conclusion. This intuitive awareness is often accompanied by a strong feeling of certainty that this knowledge, arising out of apparent nothingness, is absolutely correct.

All the words we use to describe knowing something without knowing how we know it refer to intuition. Results that seem miraculous can occur when we let intuition do its work without interference.

When we approach the angel sentinel of the intuition passageway, we find that in order to enter this passageway we must let go of our attachment to the idea that human knowledge, rationality, and facts are the only reliable way to Truth. Choosing this passageway involves the possibility of failure. Many who have entered it find they risk credibility with their colleagues or clients because of the unproveable nature of the information they receive by listening to intuition. It is only when one can repeatedly demonstrate sound intuition that produces measurable results that an idiosyncratic approach may be tolerated. I say "tolerated" because even brilliant results may not lead to being embraced by one's colleagues or friends if those results challenge the status quo upon which rests the current stature and credibility of those colleagues, or the beliefs upon which our friends have built their lives.

On occasion, I read in reputable publications that there is evidence favoring possible solutions to world problems that our government, military, or medical establishment fails to research or look into in any open way. Why might such research be avoided even though the evidence for the healing of disease, easing of suffering, or benefit to the environment could be substantial? Perhaps the supposed evidence is more faulty than its supporters would have us believe, or perhaps the risk of actively researching such ideas is perceived to be too great by those who would have to live with the consequences of having chosen to investigate.

I believe that we are not here to do what has already been done, or what we already know how to do. In order to do what has not yet been done, and what we do not know how to do, we must be willing to risk what we now have and know. Facts and knowledge are important and useful—up to a point. Our collective knowledge encompasses what is currently known or believed to be true. That type of knowledge loses its usefulness, however, when it stops us from exploring further because we fear taking the risks of failure or loss of professional credibility.

This is what we all do. We protect our own reputation, credibility, and the gains we've already made in life. This is very understandable, but it is tragic when our refusal to explore unusual or unexpected information limits our lives because we are unable to face the consequences of the changes we'd have to weather if the clues we are seeing are correct. Galileo questioned an assumption based on Aristotle's theory relating to the nature of gravity, a theory that had never been tested in the two thousand years since it was postulated. Aristotle believed that if two objects were dropped from a great height, the heavier one would reach the ground first. Galileo climbed to the top of the Tower of Pisa, and with scientists witnessing the experiment, dropped two spheres, one heavy and one light, from the top of the tower. They landed on the ground at the same time. All of the scientists present witnessed the result, but so strong was their attachment to the status quo of science as they had known it for so long, that they denied what they had seen. They continued to say and teach that Aristotle had been correct. This did not happen because Galileo's research or demonstration was faulty but because the cost to science as it was known at that time was perceived to be too great. Scientists denied what was before their eyes, not wanting to be associated with such controversy and desperately wanting to hold back the tide of progress so that they wouldn't have to throw out so much of what they'd come to assume was true, and begin again.

The chaos that resulted from Galileo's astronomical discoveries eventually caused the Catholic Church to excommunicate him. His discoveries had both theological and scientific implications that destroyed the previous paradigms of both institutions.

This pattern has interesting implications in our own lives as well. We, too, would rather avoid letting go of our familiar, comfortable ways of thinking and living. But creation doesn't stand still. We have to adapt to new developments, either now or later. When our own inner knowing—intuition—directs us to respond to life in a new way, it is because that new way is best suited to who we are and what is coming next for us in life—something we can't possibly predict. Being prepared to flow with change may make life feel less chaotic when our previous way of viewing life is blown asunder, but only if we can allow ourselves to consider the information that intuition brings.

People often ask me, "Rev. Mary, how do I know when the urge I have to do something is the Guidance of intuition, and when it's habit, ego, or some other self-centered motivation?" I wish I had an ironclad answer for that wonderful question. One way we find the answer is by listening and responding to the prompting we feel, and carefully observing what results are produced by doing so. If we are responding to Guidance, the long-term results will be better than we might have imagined, and bring benefit to more people than ourselves alone. If, on the other hand, we are responding to ego, habit, or selfish motivation, the long-term results will be mixed, creating disharmony and chaos along with enjoyment, and this situation will not easily straighten itself out over time. This is not an immediate way of knowing the difference between Guidance and ego, but an ongoing personal experiment. Another way of looking into the difference is to examine our own motivation. If that which we feel motivated to do is good for us and harmful to none, there is no reason we shouldn't go ahead with it. If we have any hope or intention of causing pain or difficulty to another person, directly or indirectly, with what we want to do, intuitive Guidance isn't what is directing that action.

When we hang on to the need to back up all actions with facts, we pass up our intuitive Guidance because we're afraid it's too risky to follow. On the other hand, when we give up the need to have a measurable, verifiable guarantee of rightness before acting, we step into the passageway that is living by intuition. The angel sentinel gives us the Quality of Being tool of intuition—our direct link for listening to the Divine Feminine within us at all times. Practicing that listening without agenda is what it means to become open to intuitive Guidance. One of the rewards of this practice is that we become proficient at catching ourselves at our own game. No longer can we easily fool ourselves into thinking that ego-motivated choices are arising from our intuition. We will have discovered through practice and trial and error what the character and content of the inner intuitive voice sounds like. We will recognize true messages more of the time, and come to trust them more easily. The result in our lives is that we become more fully responsive to the genuine Guidance that is available to every human being. We may even find ourselves in an entirely new realm of creativity.

When the Guidance of the Divine Feminine began to show up in my life as intuition, I didn't know what it was. I began to think of the experience as "It." It appeared intermittently in my life. Always unexpected, unbidden, at least by my conscious self, and always in nonlinear fashion, It revealed information, pushed me into realms of knowing I couldn't explain, and made it impossible for me to do things in the planned, intellectual fashion with which I was most comfortable.

When I began my first ministry in northern California, it began to happen as I gave my talk at the two Sunday morning services. As I spoke, examples and further explanations would appear in my head that related to my topic for the day and my point at that moment. These were not on my mind map, the organizational format I used to prepare my talks, and at first I ignored them and pushed them away. The intrusions unnerved me and made me nervous. But as they continued, I began to include them as I spoke each week. Invariably when I did they provided a much richer talk than the one I had down on paper.

It showed up, too, in my teaching. As I was teaching the curriculum for church classes on religious philosophy, examples, stories, and even class exercises would come to mind unbidden. I began to trust these and include them as they arose. Pastoral counseling sessions also became an opportunity for It to appear. As I sat with a congregant and listened to his story I would be prompted to ask questions or make comments that sometimes seemed to bear little relationship to the information he had given me. Or I would have sudden ideas of how to offer possibilities about what was happening in his life in spiritual terms that had never before occurred to me. I learned to trust all these bursts of intuition or inspiration and to share them with my congregants as they arose. This practice served me well, for there have been times I've been called to be with people when only intuitive Guidance could have helped me know what to say or do.

Early in my ministry, I was asked by a family to come over and sit with one of their loved ones who was in crisis. His alcoholism had culminated in a violent episode the night before, and although no one had been hurt, he had isolated himself in part of the house and refused to communicate with anyone. The family members were at their wit's end. Knowing their dear one trusted me, they asked me to come and talk with him. I remember driving to his house without a sense of how safe I would be with this man. All I could do was pray that I would know what to say and do once I was with him in order to help bring healing into the situation. From the moment I agreed to go until I left that home hours later I was in a constant state of willingness to be directed from the Infinite. The entire meeting was peaceful and honest, and when I left I felt I had been protected and that the gentleman I'd gone to see had also been protected from the destructiveness of his own despair. He agreed to go into an alcohol treatment program that very day.

In crisis situations, the benefit of our practice of opening to intuitive Guidance is that we can sometimes know how to respond to a situation, even when the knowing comprises information we couldn't possibly arrive at in any linear way. Additionally, in such circumstances our felt sense of knowing can be rooted in such deep certainty and willingness that we need no additional motivation or outside confirmation to act effectively.

Accessing our innate intuition requires time, belief, practice, and the willingness to set aside our attachment to rationality and logic. Some ways we can practice opening to the Quality of Being of intuition are:

- When you feel challenged in life by a conflict with another person, or a circumstance you feel unable to change, sit down and practice deep relaxation. Imagine yourself alone in a beautiful, quiet place, with plenty of time. Imagine putting the conflict (not the other person, just the conflict) into a hot air balloon basket. In your mind's eye, cut the ropes holding the basket to earth, and let it float away into space. Watch it until it disappears. Breathe deeply. After a few moments, allow the hot air balloon to reappear and descend slowly to the earth near you. Inside, the conflict has disappeared and has been replaced by the solution to the problem. Look into the basket and see what the solution is. Take it out. It may be obvious or symbolic. If obvious, ask yourself if you are willing to take the steps indicated. If symbolic, allow yourself to honor what your own inner wisdom has brought you. Ask inwardly for clarity about what this symbol means. Remain open to further information. Be sure to turn your attention to real help, rather than continuing to obsess about the problem.

- When you face a decision that is difficult, first be still and listen. Genuinely request Guidance for the best choice. Don't edit or discount what comes. Consider the Guidance fully and evaluate it based on your sense of your motivations, your hopes for the outcome following the decision, and your pull to respond by taking action. When you do act, observe the results carefully. Have you increased peacefulness or chaos? Have you magnified separation or affirmed oneness? Have you taken a stand for excellence or carelessness? Have you led with your heart, your head, or given yourself time to listen to both of them?

- When a hunch appears that feels right, test it out. Go in the direction of the hunch and see what the results are. When they're positive, file that experience away to be your guide for when to act on feelings around future hunches.

Intuition is a powerful pipeline of energy and information that flows more fully as we use what comes through it to us. Just as ongoing physical exercise increases our muscular strength, trusting our intuition repeatedly makes our intuitive ability stronger and our performance of the skill more trustworthy. Life is far too complicated for us to believe we have the ability to understand and figure out a meaningful response to everything that comes our way. The Divine Feminine becomes a valuable ally via our intuition to help us bring into our awareness more of what we need to know in order to take responsible, effective action in a timely way.

Thirteen

Gratitude

....

The day of my spiritual awakening was the day I saw—and
knew I saw—all things in God and God in all things.
                                        —*Mechtild of Magdeburg*

Gratitude, our next Quality of Being, is the knowing experience of appreciation. When we savor a delicious food,
when we admire beautiful flowers and enjoy their fragrance,
when the blend of instruments or voices in a concert lifts our
heart and makes us laugh or weep, we are immersed in gratitude, even if unknowingly. When we bring our awareness to
the level of delight we are experiencing at that moment, we are

living in a moment of gratitude and grace. Grace is sometimes described as an unearned blessing—one that comes unpredictably—that surprises, delights, refreshes, and comforts the recipient. We invite the experience of grace when we embrace the practice of gratitude.

In times of crisis, it is not only coming through the darkness that requires our gratitude but paradoxically—in a way that only people who have come out of profound darkness can understand—the darkness itself.

In a neighboring county this fall, I attended a gathering of women who had been featured on a local radio program entitled *Women of Courage.* The program's successful three-year run had yielded many inspiring interviews, and on this day the women and their guests had gathered to celebrate the strength of the human spirit in those who had overcome great challenges. I was struck by a powerful, slender, woman of color who stood and said, "I am not a victim. There have only been blessings in my life, because in God there is nothing but blessing. So the incest was a blessing; the beatings were a blessing; the rape was a blessing. They have helped make me the woman I am today. And I am proud to be who I am."

When I spoke with her after the program, I told this woman how much her sharing had moved me, and how empowering her vision of her life was—much more so than holding on to the idea that one is a victim. "Yes," she said, "but you need to be a victim first, before you can be empowered."

What I understood her to mean was that it doesn't seem we

can go to empowerment directly from the experience of being a victim, but if we go through the experience completely and come out the other side, the transformation can be awesome. It is there that gratitude and empowerment can begin.

The Divine Feminine is in constant celebration of the awe of creation. It is natural to the Divine Feminine to appreciate the beauty and complexity of the world around us and the way in which we are constantly supported and provided for by the Universe. This capacity for appreciation and receptivity is within all of us. Yet when I ask students in my church classes which is easier, giving or receiving, giving is the clear winner. Perhaps most of us find it easier to give to others than to receive—whether from the universe or from other people—because when we are giving we feel we are in control, and when we receive we are not. Being in a receptive posture can feel like a vulnerable, uncomfortable place.

In order to enter into the Quality of Being of gratitude, we are stopped by the angel sentinel at the gate to that passageway of spiritual maturity and directed to release our craving for more. The question may arise, "But Rev. Mary, *how* do I let the craving go?" One way is by intentionally embracing gratitude, not with mere lip service to it but by taking the time and making the effort to search out real reasons for gratefulness right now.

In America, we are constantly stimulated to buy products; to feel the need and desire for them; to whet our appetites for more. But sometimes we don't need *more,* we need to let in what we already have. Truly savoring the people, experiences, and things in our lives can be a full banquet—we needn't get any more to experience contentment and gratitude. The secret is to learn how to bring our attention back, with thankfulness, to what is. This practice brings life to our relationships, creative ideas to our work, and feelings of deep genuine satisfaction to our daily lives.

Practicing gratitude can have surprising results. Gratitude begins to show us things we had overlooked for a long time. Most of us, for example, have many good people and things in our lives, and it is likely that when these friends and things first came into our lives, we were thrilled by them. We saw the uniqueness they brought and appreciated the gifts they were to us in our lives. But over time, they became familiar, and became woven into the everyday fabric of our lives. When that happened, it is likely we began to overlook the blessings we initially treasured. We forgot how their presence enhanced our lives. In other words, we took them for granted.

When we apply appreciation to anything in our lives, we increase its occurrence. Don't take my word for it; try it and see. More gifts appear when we remember to treasure the ones we already have, and no matter how difficult our lives may be, we all have things for which we can be grateful. Start right now with the things that surround you as you read this page. Stop and look around you. What is nearby that you can be grateful for in this moment? Your grandchildren? Your beloved cat? The fragrance of spring? Take a moment to realize what the things or people near you are contributing to your life right this second: a feeling of love, comfort, or joy; the enjoyment of beauty. Take a moment to feel how blessed you are to have them.

I believe there is always something for which we can be grateful. It may be difficult to find and hard to feel in the midst of a dark time, but experiencing gratitude can be the beginning of a way out of the darkness, even when we are appreciating the loss of something we really wanted. Country-western star Garth Brooks sings about a married man and his wife who run into his old high school flame—a girl the man was desperately in love with at one time. But meeting her again the man becomes aware of how much he has changed over the years. "Sometimes I thank God for unanswered prayers," Garth sings. He goes on to encourage us in the song to remember that unanswered prayers are sometimes God's finest gifts. This is the type of hindsight that can teach us to appreciate tough times in life that don't make sense to us while they're happening.

When we live from gratitude, we experience our lives as happier and more complete than when we don't. Studies have shown that optimists live longer, healthier lives than pessimists. Practicing gratitude can prepare us to deal with our challenges with more humor and less stress. Coming upon the idea of practicing appreciation when we are already in challenge can seem like a mockery or minimizing of what we're experiencing. Yet if we can do it, we may get a glimmer of understanding of the deeper value of our painful experience.

It is said that when Gandhi was imprisoned he once

thanked a guard who gave him a lice-infested prison uniform to wear. Gandhi focused on the spiritual growth he believed would come from meeting the challenge of the terrible uniform with love and compassion. He thanked the guard for making that growth possible. It may be difficult to imagine being grateful for such a thing, but perhaps the example can help reveal a fresh perspective regarding unrecognized blessings in our own lives.

We're all familiar with the everyday miracle of a caterpillar becoming a butterfly. We go through similar transformations as we move through life: from childhood to adolescence, from adolescence to adulthood, from adulthood to old age. When we bring attention to these changes with gratitude we expand our current experiences of good.

Once we begin to practice gratitude, two other transformational possibilities reveal themselves. The first possibility shows up when we see a way of living that is fuller and freer than our present life, and we become grateful for that possible future in advance, before we have it. We live each day claiming the new truth with surrender and gratitude, and our efforts result in a profound change in how we think, make choices, and live. The convict who becomes a drug rehabilitation counselor; the alcoholic who becomes a motivational teacher; the parent with low self-esteem who learns how to be an outspoken advocate for her learning-disabled child—these are examples of transformation of personal lives resulting from vision coupled with gratitude. Imagine a caterpillar turning into not a butterfly but a unicorn—an *amazing* transformation. This transformation is demonstrated by the person who triumphs over an unusually difficult situation to live a richer, more satisfying life.

The second transformational possibility is even more astonishing. It is exemplified by people who envision and believe in a better life for others and who live their lives immersed in that vision with profound gratitude for its possibility. Their actions in the world, born of this huge vision and gratitude for it, create inspiration and improvements for thousands of people. These folks seem to want very little for themselves personally. Somehow they move beyond the pull of their own needs. Their focus is on connection with other people and their opportunity to relieve pain and increase happiness.

Mother Teresa, Martin Luther King, Jr., and Mohandas Gandhi are some of the people who come to mind when I think of the third kind of transformation. Theirs is the type of gratitude and faith that I imagine the master teacher Jesus was expressing when he stood at the tomb of Lazarus, who had been buried for three days. Jesus first *thanked God for hearing him,* then said, "Lazarus, come forth." These leaders exemplify what I call miraculous transformation—from the unicorn back to the caterpillar. Their own lives are simple and ordinary in appearance, but what they do is not. Behind their ordinary appearance is an extraordinary and glorious consciousness of oneness with all humanity. When we read about their lives, we find that these amazing individuals grew into this consciousness gradually—they were not born anointed or specially blessed. They had to deal with their lives and find their way just as we do. To grow into the greater awareness, their stories tell us that such leaders first had to manage their own life transitions, then go on to find a better way to live for themselves, then take a giant leap to apply what they'd learned to the larger community of humanity.

Miraculous transformation appears to be a profound leap—and it is—but it doesn't happen all at once. Though miraculous transformation may be more potent than what most of us personally experience or have the courage to express, the potential is within us all. Perhaps today each one of us is called to go beyond the usual transformative passages of life. If we are to succeed in meeting the expanding demands of our world, gratitude combined with vision is the key.

We have accelerated the pace of our lives through science and technology to such a degree that everyday changes—the normal transformations or passages we all go through in living life—simply are not enough to ensure the continuity of future generations. I believe we are called to go further, to transform ourselves beyond the common changes if we are to contribute useful wisdom for meeting the challenges, and even threats, our brilliant technology poses to our own physical and spiritual survival in the world. We must now learn to go from the caterpillar stage to the butterfly in the usual way, and then beyond that transformation to the mythic proportions of the unicorn. To do this, we must face our own fears and overcome them; we must face our own limitations and acknowledge and embrace them. I believe we will have to move beyond our natural caterpillar consciousness, which wants to stay in the cocoon and have life remain comfortably familiar. Caterpillar consciousness wants to dwell in the realm of the known. Paradoxically, in spite of our attachment to the known, when we operate like the caterpillar we rarely appreciate what surrounds us—we are too preoccupied with hanging on to it.

"Be ye transformed by the renewing of your minds," said St. Paul, implying that a changed attitude of mind is the *essential element* in the transformational process. This renewing of the mind is at the heart of the transformative power of combining gratitude with vision, whether for ourselves personally or for the larger community of humanity.

Here are two stories of personal transformations that were born of vision and gratitude in advance for the possibility of a healed life. In both instances the gratitude that was born with the vision continued unabated throughout the subject's life following the healing.

The first is a story told by Norman Vincent Peale about his father's ministry. A congregant who had a reputation as a drunk and a wife beater came forward during an altar call at the church. Rev. Peale, Sr., put his hand on the man's head, and the kneeling congregant asked for prayer. "Please pray for me, Reverend, I don't want to be this way anymore." So the minister prayed. When the gentleman arose his face shone, but no one in the church expected his "conversion" to last. It did, though, along with the man's shining face, for many years right up to his death. This fellow became an active church leader and a role model in the congregation. His change went beyond not drinking—a butterfly kind of change. This caterpillar was transformed into a unicorn. The faith of a unicorn is greatly increased and expanded when his hopeful vision and his feeling of gratitude are confirmed by the manifestation of what he has envisioned. After this transformative experience, his way of being and of taking action in the world are profoundly changed.

The story of how the song "Amazing Grace" came to be concerns another caterpillar who became a unicorn, and once again the combination of vision and gratitude were key. A slave ship captain was called to address a problem in the hold of his vessel. His ship's cargo—hundreds of African men, women, and children being transported to be sold—had become ill during the rough crossing in the terrible darkness and filth of the conditions below deck. When the captain looked down into the hold at them to consider what needed to be done, he was surprised to discover that instead of seeing cargo, for the first time he saw suffering human beings. He turned the ship around to take them home, went to his cabin to pray for forgiveness, and penned this song: "Amazing grace, how sweet the sound, that saved a wretch like me. / I once was lost, but now I'm found; was blind, but now I see."

In listening to the song we can hear and feel his gratitude in the lyric, "how sweet the sound that saved a wretch like me." The captain felt overwhelming gratitude for the ability to finally see the truth and reclaim his own lost humanity. To him, this awareness was born of grace—a blessing he felt he could not possibly have deserved.

The story of the captain's transformation seldom accompanies the singing of this wonderful hymn, yet people still cry when they hear the song because the depth of change that took place in the man is communicated and felt, even without the history of how the song came to be.

Miraculous transformation, the third possibility revealed by gratitude, describes the accomplishments of Martin Luther King, Jr., Gandhi, and Mother Teresa—accomplishments that go beyond the hopes, fears, and aspirations of the average person. Their lives and words were more than thought provoking, they were heart stirring. We borrowed their visions and gratitude. We leaned against their strength. Their eloquence communicated itself to us so deeply we felt they were speaking directly to us. They were people like us, but with more courage, more patience, more clarity.

In the course of their lifetimes, each of these leaders grew into something more than she or he appeared to be on the outside. Each one approached life with a deep sense of gratitude and reverence, and a commitment to seeing beyond appearances to what could be, as well as to what already existed in seed form in the existing conditions. Their gratitude, their vision, and their steadiness were powerfully communicated to us through their actions, which mirrored their words so beautifully. When Gandhi said "My life is my message," he summarized not only his own life's work but that of these others who, like himself, lift our eyes to a greater possibility. King's vision of equality and dignity for all people; Gandhi's commitment to civil disobedience and nonviolence; Mother Teresa's ability to see the Presence of God in every person she met—these consistent, able people, and their tireless efforts to live as the transformational fire that had ignited them, show us what it means to go beyond the transformations that empower us to re-create our own lives with visions that empower our communities as well.

In this third type of transformation, the one in which such leaders exemplify transformation in which the unicorn becomes a caterpillar again, the caterpillar is no ordinary insect, although it looks just like the others. Something has returned it to its original appearance, but this caterpillar's way of seeing and responding to the world is entirely different from its earlier version. The Zen saying "Before enlightenment, chop wood and carry water; after enlightenment, chop wood and carry water," summarizes this phenomenon. The idea of chopping wood and carrying water—the same activity before and after enlightenment—emphasizes that the difference is not in the outer form of the task or the worker, which remains the same before and after the transformation. The difference is in the inner experience of the one performing the tasks. Daily life for the unicorn turned caterpillar may look just like the old life, but its meaning to him is entirely different.

In order for any one of us to live life from this exalted consciousness, the question put to us by the Divine Feminine is, "Are you willing to be changed at depth?" This question demands more of us than merely to release our craving for more and to learn to be grateful in the moment. It asks us to open to a vision for other people and to appreciate and courageously work toward the possibility revealed in that vision. Gratitude, as a quality of the Divine Feminine, is expressed as delighting in the beauty and flow and goodness of life just as it is. It is looking beyond our traditional judgment of appearances as good/bad, beautiful/ugly, desirable/undesirable.

Once this practice has been established, the second phase of gratitude requires stepping beyond our personal limitations. We catch a glimpse of a larger possibility for ourselves, and we claim that vision with hope and appreciation. Eventually we become grateful even for apparently unpleasant experiences of our own lives. When a relative is alcoholic, when a child is rebellious, when we lose our home, it is difficult to see these people and situations as the source of potential benefit. In order to approach people and situations in our life with the assumption that their presence is always a blessing, we must look beyond appearances when the conditions or behavior of the moment do not seem to bring us benefit in the traditional sense.

Try these practices of gratitude:

- Acknowledge people at home or at work for things they've done, their natural beauty, their sense of humor—anything you enjoy or appreciate about them (this requires *noticing*). This practice of gratitude feeds others and nourishes our relationships with them. It is especially effective with children—kids thrive on attention.

- Recognize your current abilities and freedoms. W. Mitchell, an inspirational professional speaker who was severely burned in a motorcycle crash and rendered paraplegic after a plane accident, describes the practice this way. "I used to be able to do ten thousand things. Now I can do only nine thousand. I prefer to pay attention to the nine thousand things I *can* do, rather than the one thousand I can't."

- Feel what your body can do. Our bodies are miracles of flexibility and healing power. Usually we don't notice them much as long as everything is working well and going smoothly. Rather than waiting for a health challenge to bring your attention to your body, begin to notice and marvel at it now: the physical feelings of heat, cold, pressure, hunger, stretching; the experience of emotions: excitement, sorrow, joy, delight, anger, fear, affection; the senses you enjoy: sight, hearing, taste, touch, smell; the ability to move, think, and create: to walk, dance, ride a bike, write a poem, tie your shoes.

If we persist with our practice of gratitude we move into the third phase: opening to a larger vision for our family and our community and taking steps to bring that vision into being. Living that vision can lead us into outrageous transformation. Ernest Holmes wrote in *A Time for Thanksgiving,* "It will perform a miracle in your life if you consciously bless every situation you find yourself in."

Fourteen

Trust

....

"Come to the edge of the cliff," he said.
"We're afraid," they said.
"Come to the edge of the cliff," he said.
"We're afraid," they said.
 They came.
 He pushed.
 They flew.

Guillaume Appollinaire

When we have passed through the previously described passageways in our personal transformative darkness, and have been cautioned by the angel sentinels there to release what we are carrying and receive the next attitudinal gift to practice, we find the light at the end of the tunnel has become quite bright, and we are about to step out into it. At that moment, if we are ready, we may find there is yet another sentinel to pass. This is the angel who extends the tool of trust. Trust is both a prerequisite for, and a result of, practicing the other Qualities of Being. When we fully embrace the gift of trust, we never can go back to the old way of seeing our lives.

This angel whispers, "Let go of your need for things to be different than they are. In order to live in trust you must be willing to weather change, walk through fear, work through anger to forgiveness, let brokenness become your healing, and live through death." To enable us do all these things we practice the Qualities of Being in our daily lives and at times of crisis, and in this way, the little trust with which we begin becomes stronger and grows.

Trust is a huge step. Saints around us may manage to let go into the Divine Feminine completely, becoming our source of inspiration and motivation, but most of us live our lives only in partial trust. The Divine Feminine exists in an atmosphere of ultimate trust. Being one, indivisible Presence, the Divine Feminine within and around us has nothing to lose or fear. It lacks nothing. As we become more aware of that Presence within us as part of our own essential makeup we find it easier to release fear and embrace the unknown with increasing trust, realizing that we, too, are connected to all that is in a vast whole.

Evelyn, a woman friend of vast life experience, has been a particular inspiration to me in the way she trusts the Infinite. I remember sitting and talking with her six years ago when she was about seventy. Evelyn had married young, raised her children, divorced, lived in an ashram following a guru, completed her college education as a senior citizen, and was working as a psychotherapist for people with life-threatening illnesses. Her life had been full of the most joyful and fulfilling work, and she had not been afraid to begin any of it, she said. Not long ago, I made a comment in her presence about the universal human experience of, and belief in the necessity of, aging. Evelyn, exuding love and peacefulness as always, smiled sweetly, and said to me, "Don't ever believe in age, Mary."

She once told me that years earlier when her marriage was ending her husband had said to her, "I always thought that someday you'd grow up and stop changing!" Thank God she never has. Evelyn's ability to embrace life and all of its changes inspires me to more fully trust the twists and turns in my own.

When we live in trust, we find a greater awareness and discovery of who we are. We re-create ourselves anew, from the discoveries we make as we grow, rendering our lives *full* — useful and meaningful. In a song he co-wrote, "My Connection with God," a friend and colleague of mine, Dr. Michael Beckwith, says, "We ended up with a sense of filled-full-ment, but never with that deep sense of fulfillment." Fulfillment, contentment in life, peacefulness — now in the middle of my life I find myself more interested in these than in the excitement, fame, fortune, and status that drew my ambitious heart in younger years. It seems I've realized that maintaining the latter values is exhausting, while the former give me energy. I can choose contentment at any moment, no matter what the circumstances. There are no prerequisites to its existence. This awareness is very freeing and is one of the benefits of practicing living in trust.

In order to live in trust we have to let go of waiting for things to change before we enjoy our lives. Subtly we put off so many things until what we imagine will be the exact right moment: "I'll take a vacation *after* I . . ." "I'll forgive her *when* she . . ." "I'd feel better *if* . . ." "I'll start investing money *as soon as* . . ." "I'll begin tithing *once* I've got . . ." By making our trust in the Infinite dependent upon circumstances, we put off discovering the bliss of opening up to divine developments in our life today. This is what I mean by partial trust. We mean to trust once we feel a little more secure. But ironically, the way to trust is to begin in uncertainty. Beginning where we are, rather than waiting until we achieve some arbitrary benchmark, allows the resources of the Universe to respond to us now. If we don't trust now, we will only substitute other prerequisites once those we now use to excuse our lack of trust have been fulfilled. Trust will be eternally put off, and so will its blessings.

The Divine Feminine in us is the deepening of our trust in, and awareness of, our Oneness with the Infinite Source of all. The Divine Feminine around us is that atmosphere of being and consciousness that somehow communicates to us that we are loved and safe always, regardless of conditions.

Trust is not only for the moments we let go and things turn

out well. We may decide an outcome is positive because it is one that feels good and of which we approve—one that we understand and with which we agree. Some outcomes will not look or feel like what we want or understand. These are the crucial times to practice trust. Ram Dass, in his study of Eastern religions, summed up the mystery and paradox of our partial information this way, "It's beautiful; it stinks. There's nothing to do; do it."

The outer forms of our lives may not change at all as our spiritual maturity, acceptance, and understanding deepen, but how we experience these same forms can become dramatically different as we grow in spiritual insight. And even when the outer forms do change, we may still find ourselves returning to them eventually, only to discover that while the old forms are the same, we ourselves have changed profoundly owing to the practice of trust.

Another story from Ram Dass illustrates this idea beautifully. During check-in time in the dormitory of a meditation retreat, Ram Dass met the man who would be bunking above him. They began to talk. "What do you do?" Ram Dass asked the man. "I'm the vice president of industrial loans for a bank," he replied. "Really!" said Ram Dass. "How do you happen to be attending this meditation retreat?" "Well," the man responded, "in the sixties, I was vice president of industrial loans for the bank, and it looked like everyone was having more fun than I was. So I quit my job, left my family, and went into the mountains. I threw pots and took drugs. I learned to meditate.

Then one day I was in the city and I ran into the president of the bank. 'Funny I should run into you,' he said to me. 'Your job is available again. And you were the best vice president of industrial loans I ever had. How about coming back to work?' " The man went on, "I thought, 'Why not?' So, I bought a tie and went back to work." "And is it any different now than it was when you were doing it before?" Ram Dass asked the man. "Oh, it's entirely different!" the man replied. "Before, I was the vice president of industrial loans. Now, I go to this place and hang out with these people all day long, and the *vehicle* for my being with them is industrial loans."

In case this example is too "sixties" to be understood by those who weren't there, let me interpret. Once this gentleman had taken the time to step out of his regular routine and habitual way of seeing the world, he discovered new ways to respond and new possibilities for connection with others. When he returned to the routine of bank work, he found his experience of those old things had changed. The routine and the bank employees had not changed, but his way of coming to them and seeing them had changed. Where he previously saw only an unfulfilling job, now he saw his relationship to the people he encountered as paramount, and his work as the vehicle for bringing him together with others. The interactions were now precious, whereas before they were mundane.

While I am not advocating abandoning one's family to transform one's point of view, sometimes the universe takes us through amazing, unpredictable, and sometimes unsettling changes in our circumstances, thereby bringing us to a fuller perspective. Trusting those changes when they come can bring us tremendous blessings and richness that extend out from us to the people our lives touch.

The Divine Feminine operates in utter trust. Its natural expression is one of complete safety and the ability to let go and creatively express all that is pressing forward to be expressed without fear. When we stop thinking that we have to put off the calling of our heart until we accomplish something "important," we are free to experience and express the Divine impulsion within us. The practice of trust is a moment-by-moment unfoldment. It increases the voice of the Divine Feminine in our experience because the practice of trust, like the practice of intuition, heightens our receptivity to that voice.

Living in trust establishes us as rooted and grounded in the Divine. Life's ups and downs affect us, but they don't pitch us off course for long. When trust is our daily practice, the dark moments of life cause us to go deeper into our practice. Trust allows us to look at the appearance of the challenge that faces us and, regardless of what it looks like, to let go into the flow of God, knowing the activity of God is unfolding perfectly, and we can choose peacefulness even when others think we should choose despair. There can be great peace in feeling that we are part of a harmonious unfoldment of good even in moments of our greatest pain and anguish.

Living in trust can be practiced in the following ways:

- Stop putting off the activities you'd like to explore until things get better. Enjoy your life right now.
- Begin to repair damaged relationships now. If you value those interpersonal connections, don't wait until a family crisis or the meltdown of someone's marriage to try listening and forgiveness.
- Plan to create memories rather than spending money on consumables that are soon gone. Do special things. Visit places you've always wanted to see. Don't be like the hypothetical man Dr. Paul Pearson describes in his book *The Heart's Code,* who comes to the end of his life and has inscribed on his tombstone, "Got everything done. Died anyway."

Daily we are given opportunities to trust Guidance in the simplest things. "Should I eat a snack?" "Should I leave early for the meeting or finish this correspondence?" "Should I tell my wife the truth about this?" Most often our active response to these internal questions is motivated by habit and fear rather than by listening for and trusting our Guidance. If you're like me, you may have experienced that often such actions add up to more of the results we're already getting. If these results work and we are content with them, there's nothing to change. But if we find that change is pressing us—that we are pulled toward going deeper and learning ways that are more connected to Divine direction than our old familiar habits—the practice of trust can give us new insights and experiences upon which to base our responses.

Afterword

As I have been writing this book, many friends, neighbors, clients, and former congregants have asked me what it is about. My usual answer has been that *Guidance from the Darkness* is about how shattering challenges in our lives can be the gateway to transformation. In many cases, the person who has asked the question has nodded knowingly at that answer. Somehow we know that challenges can lead to profound

change. While we wouldn't have chosen the pain we experienced in the past if we had known how to avoid it, having
come through it successfully we seem to see how it contributed
to our lives in magnificent and unpredictable ways, because
the crisis changed us for the better. It doesn't take a special
kind of person to have this experience, just a special way of
looking at and responding to life.

In our journey together we have explored some of the most
challenging of human emotions and experiences: change, fear,
anger, loss, and death. We have seen how looking at these experiences from a positive viewpoint—expecting good to come
from them even when we can't see how—can lead to greater
health, peace, possibilities, and freedom. We have also learned
that we can enjoy our everyday lives more fully right now,
while preparing ourselves for future challenges, by practicing
the Qualities of Being: attention, intention, choice, practice,
surrender, intuition, gratitude, and trust. While ongoing practice of the Qualities requires that we let familiar attitudes and
behaviors go, it teaches that the adoption of new attitudes and
behaviors can permanently develop us and our way of living
into strong, resilient, visionary leaders.

It has been my pleasure to share these ideas with you. I
hope *Guidance from the Darkness* has helped you to find that
new way of seeing and responding. Perhaps the most appropriate way to end our time together is to share with you the
Sanskrit greeting used in India and Nepal when people meet
and when they part. They press the palms of their hands to-

gether at heart level and bow to one another, saying *"Namaste,"* one translation of which is "the God in me bows to the God in you." But my favorite translation of the greeting is this: "I honor that place in you where the entire universe resides. I honor the place where when you are in that place in you, and I am in that place in me, there is only One." Blessings on your journey. *Namaste.*

Permissions

....

About the Author

....

The Reverend Mary Murray Shelton, a Religious Science minister, is a founding member of the Sacred Arts Council and instructor in the Holmes Institute School of Ministry. She has served on the International Board of Trustees for the United Church of Religious Science, and is a gifted speaker and teacher who leads women's retreats and workshops and speaks to organizations and at conferences across the country.

These exciting titles in Tarcher's New Thought Library
are available from your favorite book retailer.